VOLUME ONE
ISSUE TWO
JULY 2005

CULTURAL
POLITICS

AIMS AND SCOPE

Cultural Politics is an international, refereed journal that explores the global character and effects of contemporary culture and politics. *Cultural Politics* explores precisely what is *cultural* about politics and what is *political* about culture. Publishing across the Arts, Humanities and Social Sciences, the journal welcomes articles from different political positions, cultural approaches and geographical locations.

Cultural Politics publishes work that analyses how cultural identities, agencies and actors, political issues and conflicts, and global media are linked, characterized, examined and resolved. In so doing, the journal supports the innovative study of established, embryonic, marginalised or unexplored regions of cultural politics.

Cultural Politics, while embodying the interdisciplinary coverage and discursive critical spirit of contemporary cultural studies, emphasizes how cultural theories and practices intersect with and elucidate analyses of political power. The journal invites articles on: representation and visual culture; modernism and postmodernism; media, film and communications; popular and elite art forms; the politics of production and consumption; language; ethics and religion; desire and psychoanalysis; art and aesthetics; the culture industry; technologies; academics and the academy; cities, architecture and the spatial; global capitalism; Marxism; value and ideology; the military, weaponry and war; power, authority and institutions; global governance and democracy; political parties and social movements; human rights; community and cosmopolitanism; transnational activism and change; the global public sphere; the body; identity and performance; heterosexual, transsexual, lesbian and gay sexualities; race, blackness, whiteness and ethnicity; the social inequalities of the global and the local; patriarchy, feminism and gender studies; postcolonialism; and political activism.

Cultural Politics invites papers comprising a broad range of subjects, methodological approaches, and historical and social events. Such papers may take the form of articles and case studies, review essays, interviews, book reviews, field reports, interpretative critiques and visual essays.

Cultural Politics enjoys an agreement with the Chinese journal *Cultural Studies*, published in Beijing, that allows selected articles to be published in both journals nearly simultaneously, thus furthering intellectual exchange between English and Chinese-speaking academicians and artists.

Typeset by JS Typesetting Ltd, Porthcawl, Mid Glamorgan
Printed in the UK

Anyone wishing to submit an article, interview, book, film or exhibition review for possible publication in this journal should contact the editors at,

j.armitage@unn.ac.uk

ellrb@nus.edu.sg

ISSN: 1743-2197

SUBSCRIPTION INFORMATION

Three issues per volume.

One volume per annum.

2005: Volume 1

ONLINE
www.bergpublishers.com

BY MAIL
Berg Publishers
C/o Customer Services
Extenza-Turpin
Pegasus Drive
Stratton Business Park
Biggleswade
Bedfordshire SG18 8TQ
UK

BY FAX
+44 (0)1767 601640

BY TELEPHONE
+44 (0)1767 604800

INQUIRIES

Editorial: Tristan Palmer, Managing Editor, email: tristanpalmereditor@yahoo.com

Production: Ian Critchley, email: icritchley@bergpublishers.com

Advertising and subscriptions: Veruschka Selbach, email: vselbach@bergpublishers.com

SUBSCRIPTION RATES

Institutions' subscription rate £150/US$250

Individuals' subscription rate £40/US$65*

*This price is available only to personal subscribers and must be prepaid by personal cheque or credit card

Free online subscription for print subscribers

Full colour images available online

Access your electronic subscription through www.ingenta.com or www.ingentaselect.com

REPRINTS FOR MAILING

Copies of individual articles may be obtained from the publishers at the appropriate fees.
Write to

Berg Publishers
1st Floor, Angel Court
81 St Clements Street
Oxford OX4 1AW
UK

CULTURAL POLITICS
VOLUME ONE
ISSUE TWO
JULY 2005

CONTENTS

CULTURAL POLITICS   VOLUME 1, ISSUE 2
PP 139–164

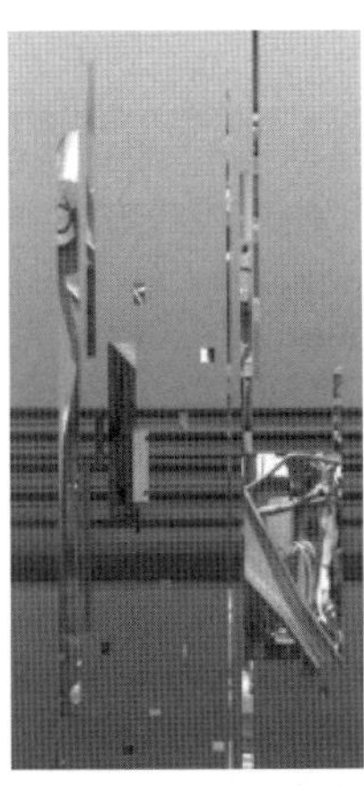

THE CONSERVATIVE ASSAULT ON AMERICA: CULTURAL POLITICS, EDUCATION AND THE NEW AUTHORITARIANISM

HENRY A. GIROUX

HENRY A. GIROUX HOLDS THE GLOBAL TV NETWORK CHAIR IN COMMUNICATIONS AT MCMASTER UNIVERSITY IN CANADA. HIS MOST RECENT BOOKS INCLUDE: *THE ABANDONED GENERATION: DEMOCRACY BEYOND THE CULTURE OF FEAR* (PALGRAVE 2004A); COAUTHORED WITH SUSAN SEARLS GIROUX, *TAKE BACK HIGHER EDUCATION: RACE, YOUTH, AND THE CRISIS OF DEMOCRACY IN THE POST CIVIL RIGHTS ERA* (PALGRAVE MACMILLAN, 2004); AND *THE TERROR OF NEOLIBERALISM* (PARADIGM 2004B).

ABSTRACT   This article argues that while the United States has been drifting toward the ideological right since the 1980s, the election of George W. Bush marks a qualitative turn toward authoritarianism. This authoritarian turn is traced through the rise of four antidemocratic tendencies in American society: neoliberalism, religious fundamentalism, militarism and educational conformism. All these fundamentalisms will be accentuated with the reelection of George W. Bush, and most of the democratic gains of the last century will be rolled back. In opposition to this rising tide of authoritarianism, the author calls for the primacy of a cultural politics in which learning is linked to social change and pedagogy is embraced as a moral and political practice that takes place in a wide range of cultural sites.

> If this were a dictatorship, it'd be a heck of a lot easier, just so long as I'm the dictator.
>
> (George W. Bush, December 18, 2000)[1]

INTRODUCTION: MOVING RIGHT

During the late 1980s, it became clear that the U.S. government and popular will were shifting to the ideological right. From the beginning of the 1980s, President Ronald Reagan and his cohorts breathed new life into the authoritarian right, using the power of their historical bloc to wage an intense battle to weaken labor unions, dismantle the welfare state, eliminate the Department of Education, support right-wing contras in Nicaragua, and increasingly make use of the state to contain and punish marginalized groups rather than invest in eliminating poverty, racism and other factors promoting human suffering. What few people anticipated at the time was the degree to which democracy would be under siege in the decades that followed. If the 1980s belonged to Reagan and his brand of social conservatism and militarism, the 1990s belonged to Bill Clinton and a more friendly, though no less pernicious, brand of neoliberalism that placed economics above democratic politics and corporate interests above public considerations. As liberalism dropped its concern for social provisions and morphed into the bloodthirsty, Darwinian politics of neoliberalism, democratic values were subordinated to market values, and corporate interests began to shape government interests rather than be subject to their regulatory controls. Politics outside the realm of the marketplace appeared inconceivable just as neoliberalism put into place a notion of agency marked by an unbridled form of self-interest and a value system unconcerned with ethical considerations. While Clinton did not follow the imperial ambitions of his predecessor, he waged a low-intensity war at home against the poor by initiating a reactionary welfare-reform package that punished people who were poor, single mothers, and minorities of color. He also abetted the conservative initiative that had made headway in the Congress and courts in the 1980s to criminalize social problems by disinvesting in social reform and reinvesting in a state that was increasingly concerned more about punishment, containment and surveillance than addressing the underlying causes of social problems.

With the election of George W. Bush to the presidency in 2000, democracy was drastically weakened as its most basic underlying principles began to unravel. The corporate state unabashedly began to replace the last vestiges of the democratic state as the central principles of a market fundamentalism were applied with a vengeance to every aspect of society.[2] All things social as well as the very concept of the public good were under attack since they detracted from the interests of profit making and limited the expansion and possibilities of market identities, values, and relations. Consequently, those noncommodified values that are central to a democracy – liberty, justice, and equality – were either ignored or treated as irrelevant by a new type of social and economic order marked by a shift away from the old forces and values of industrial production toward a new emphasis on financial capital and the wealth generated by "immaterial" production within the new knowledge-information industries. Citizenship was now largely defined through a passive notion of choice in which buying and selling constituted the meaning and substance of individual and social agency. Within this shift in which the work ethic was replaced by the ethic of consumption, esthetics replaced civic responsibility as human needs were almost entirely subordinated to the dictates of the market and the growing spectacle of patriotic jingoism (Bauman 1998). The shift from acts of civic responsibility to the esthetics of consumerism and the spectacle of patriotism not only further devalued the rhetoric of democracy but it also equated dissent with treason and imposed democracy abroad with guns, bombs and an invading army.

Under the onslaught of market forces unleashed globally during this period, the old social contracts between labor and capital and the middle class and working poor came under increasing attack. At the same time, all levels of government were hollowed out due to the ongoing attempt on the part of neoliberal advocates to battle against any remnants of the welfare state such as its promise of minimum security through collective safety nets providing basic social services. Labor now became temporary, flexible and contingent; and the image of labor as long-term, secure, and tied to the traditional notion of the work ethic was now viewed more as a burden than an asset. Job security, always fragile at best, came under increasing attack as deregulation, downsizing, outsourcing, and flexibility reduced work everywhere to part-time and minimum-wage jobs, redundancy, and a future without a vestige of security (Bauman 2001). Flexibility became the new catchword, signaling that in the new global order nothing is fixed, permanent or secure, and that the very nature of identity and agency must be amenable to short notice, the dictates of a radical uncertainty and the whims of a market economy that appeared unchecked by the political power of the nation state. But the loss of faith in the welfare state did more than inject a radical insecurity, fear, and uncertainty into many people's lives, while increasing the hardships and suffering they experienced; it also signaled the emergence of a political revolution in which power was increasingly separated from local politics, and all the gains made during the New Deal were now under aggressive attack by an administration that made an unholy alliance between rigid advocates of neoliberal capitalism, empire-seeking neoconservatives, and a powerful group of evangelical Christians (Greider 2003).

On the domestic front, the Bush administration waged an aggressive battle for privatization, deregulation, vouchers and the destruction of all those vital public spheres wedded to providing citizens with social supports, democratic values and noncommodified ways of "organizing and deepening political, economic, and social freedom" (Unger and West 1998: 59). The obsession with privatization accompanied by an unadulterated celebration of excessive individualism and individual choices offered a rationale for implementing policies that brutally destroyed all those social relations at odds with free-market orthodoxies as well as all those noncommodified public spheres that called into question the limits of commercial culture and the politically impotent forms of democracy and citizenship it legitimated. Any institution that took seriously the democratic imperative to regenerate public life and address major social problems became a target to be commercialized, privatized, or simply eliminated. With public life being drained of any substance, it became more difficult for the public to even imagine expanding democratic possibilities and hopes. The social costs of a number of draconian policies pursued by Bush and his cronies took their toll in the hard currency of human suffering. The latest Census Bureau figures reveal that the number of Americans living in poverty jumped to 35 million in 2003 (up by 1.3 million since 2002) while the number of those without health care insurance rose to 45 million (up 1.4 million). "Hardest hit were women, who for the first time since 1999 saw their earnings decline, and children. By the end of 2003, 12.9 million children lived in poverty" (Connolly and Wittem 2004: A1). In America, 17.6 percent of children live in poverty, and the infant mortality rate increased for the first time in decades in 2002. For African-Americans, the poverty rate was "nearly twice the national rate, with 24.4 percent of blacks living below the poverty line in 2003" (Hopkins 2004). Bush's policies punished poor African-Americans, women and children but rewarded with massive tax cuts the wealthiest 1 percent of Americans, who, with incomes of $1.1 million per year, saw an average tax cut of $78,460 and saw their share of the total tax burden fall roughly 32 percentage points to 2.1 percent. The tax cuts for the wealthiest 10 percent of Americans will total $148 billion (Claxton and Hansen 2004). Commenting on Bush's tax cuts, Jim Wallis (2003), the editor of *Sojourner Magazine*, claims, "The truth is that hungry people will go without food stamps, poor children will go without health care, elderly will go without medicine, and school children will go without textbooks, so that the taxes of the wealthiest Americans can be further reduced." While the Bush administration extended tax cuts to the super rich, it scaled back a range of programs – including job training, housing, higher education, Medicaid benefits – and an array of social-services that benefit the poor and the disadvantaged. Molly

Ivins (2003) estimated that as a result of the 2004 Bush budget, 50,000 kids will be cut from after-school programs, 33,000 from child care, 8,000 homeless kids from crucial education programs, and 532,000 families from heating assistance. But while the poor suffered under the Bush presidency, the economy prospered for billionaires. As Holly Sklar (2004) points out, "The new Forbes list of the 400 richest Americans has 313 billionaires – up 51 billionaires from 262 [in 2003]."

While the state under the Bush administration was hollowed out – abdicating its power to regulate the social sphere, act as the guardian of the public interest and provide social guarantees for the needs of children, the poor and the aged – it was far from rendered inconsequential. What emerged under Bush's first term was not an impotent state, but a garrison state that increasingly protected corporate interests and glorified financial markets while stepping-up the level of repression and militarization on the domestic front. Bush's war on terrorism appeared to mimic the very forces it was fighting as it gutted civil liberties and organized civic society around a culture of fear rather than a discourse of shared responsibility and democratic values. Under a flurry of repressive legislation passed after the events of September 11, American citizens were denied any legal rights and could be detained indefinitely by the American government without due access to a lawyer, family, or friends. Needless to say, the Bush administration's contempt for law and due process emboldened those "defenders of democracy" who blithely argue against freedom in the name of providing security against potential acts of terrorism. In the name of providing security, the fear industry with its massive security system is sprouting up everywhere making it easier for the government to expand its potential for control, surveillance and just plain spying on people.[3] Seemingly indifferent to the fact that societies that offer to exchange liberty for security often end up "with neither liberty nor security" (Hitchens 2004: 8), the Bush administration used the spectacle of fear and the culture of insecurity to narrow political dialogue, escalate the forces of authoritarianism, and further promote the militarization of everyday life.

The incessant quest for homeland security took place at the same time that political debate collapsed under the weight of Bush's war on terrorism. One consequence that now shapes the present, as William Greider (2004: 14) points out, is that "the [endless] quest for homeland security is heading, in ad hoc fashion, toward the quasi militarization of everyday life." Another consequence of America's infatuation with militarization can be seen in its invasion of Iraq wrapped up in the missionary discourse of democracy brought to life in daily bombings and the unreported killing of thousands of Iraqis, a large percentage of whom are children. The hypocrisy of this contradiction is apparent in the dreadful images of American soldiers torturing detainees at Abu Ghraib prison in Iraq, which reflect not only the dark side of the debacle in Iraq, but also seem to represent a "photograph that Americans had taken of themselves – a self-portrait that refracts a collective identity whose spokespersons have conflated pre-emptive war and invasion with liberation" (Feldman 2004: 2). Brute force abroad and the fear of being unpatriotic at home set in motion – albeit with flags waving and Fox Television News blasting at full volume – a wave of fear and repression in which civil society was organized essentially for the production of violence and the shutting down of any critical opposition. Under Bush's first term as president fear and cynicism became the most powerful values shaping public life and the United States appeared to be "perilously close to becoming an Orwellian dystopia" (Eakin 2004: 9).

As power was more and more concentrated in the hands of corporate elites and the upper class, government was largely removed from the needs of most people, but especially those who were disadvantaged by virtue of their race, class, age and gender. These groups were often seen either as a political liability or as disposable. Modern democracy was increasingly subverted as public life was progressively militarized, undermined through a government-sponsored culture of fear, and financially weakened by an immoral war that drained valuable resources from social services as it also produced a $422 billion deficit. In a shameful act of ethical and political indifference to young people, the Bush administration has saddled future generations with a crippling debt and a bleak future.[4] As Hans Johnson (2004: 20) points out, "Today the nation's treasury log reads like a giant ransom note to today's children, rife with red ink from the record $422 billion deficit they will repay. And the roll call of fewer jobs, lower wages and diminished healthcare coverage revives talk of the 'misery index'."

Many youthful, critical educators in the late 1980s (including myself) viewed democracy, even with its damaged legacy, as a referent for developing political and social practices that would invigorate critical citizenship, expand the possibilities of public life, and energize an educational system that needed to recognize the valuable role it played in strengthening and extending the most important principles of a democracy to be realized. In the aftermath of the election of George W. Bush to the presidency in 2004, democracy is being threatened as at no other time in the recent past and the United States may be on the verge of surrendering its democratic ideals, practices and values to an emerging authoritarianism that is casting a heavy shadow across America at the present historical moment.[5]

THE RISE OF FOUR ANTIDEMOCRATIC TENDENCIES IN THE US

A number of powerful antidemocratic tendencies now threaten American democracy. The first is a market fundamentalism that not only trivializes democratic values and public concerns, but also enshrines a rabid individualism, an all-embracing quest for profits and a social Darwinism in which misfortune is seen as a weakness and the Hobbesian rule of a "war of all against all" replaces any vestige of shared responsibilities or compassion for others. Within neoliberal ideology, the market becomes the template for organizing the rest of society. Everybody is now a customer or client and every relationship is ultimately judged in bottom-line, cost-effective terms. Similarly, as Paul Krugman (2003: A27) points out, "The hijacking of public policy by private interests" parallels "the downward spiral in governance". With the rise of market fundamentalism, economics is accorded more respect than politics, the citizen has been reduced to a consumer and the buying and selling of goods is all that seems to matter. Even children are now targeted primarily as customers, reduced to commodities, sexualized in endless advertisements and shamelessly treated as a market for huge profits. Under such circumstances, hope is foreclosed and it becomes difficult either to imagine a life beyond capitalism or to believe in a politics that takes democracy seriously.

The second fundamentalism can be seen in a religious fervor embraced by Bush and his cohorts that not only serves up creationism instead of science but also substitutes blind faith for critical reason.[6] This is a deeply disturbing trend in which the line between the state and religion is being erased as radical Christian evangelicals embrace and impose a moralism on Americans that is largely racist, bigoted, patriarchal, uncritical, and insensitive to real social problems such as poverty, racism, the crisis in health care and the increasing impoverishment of America's children. Instead of addressing these problems, a flock of dangerous evangelicals who have enormous political clout are waging a campaign to ban same-sex marriages, privatize social security, eliminate embryonic stem-cell research and overturn *Roe v. Wade* and other abortion rights cases. Right-wing religious groups such as the Traditional Values Coalition attempt to impose their religious ideology on scientific research by influencing the awarding of individual government research grants, especially those that deal with sexuality, drug abuse and HIV/AIDS transmission. In the Republican-controlled Congress, the federal govement now finances religious projects under the guise of promoting scientific research that has nothing to do with the principles or methods of rigorous scientific work. For instance, the federal government has funded a $2.3 million project to determine whether praying promotes good health (Holt 2004: 17). A group of about sixty scientists, including twenty Nobel laureates, issued a public statement accusing the Bush administration of purposefully distorting, suppressing and abusing scientific analysis from federal agencies to promote ideologically driven policy goals. For example, the scientists charged that scientific studies about global warming were ignored by the Bush administration. Even worse, government reports were censored "to remove views not in tune with Bush's politics" (Associated Press 2004a).

A new breed of religious zealot is being elected to the highest level of government, buttressed by a media largely controlled by conservative corporate interests and a growing evangelical base of Christian fundamentalists. For instance, the newly elected Taliban-esque senator from Oklahoma, Tom Coburn, has publicly argued for the death penalty for doctors who perform abortions. Jim DeMint, the new senator from South Carolina, wants to ban gays from teaching in public schools; and Jon Thune, the newly elected senator from South Dakota, supports a constitutional amendment banning flag burning, not to mention making permanent Bush's tax cuts for the rich. Widely recognized as creating the first faith-based presidency, George W. Bush has done more during his first term to advance the agenda of right-wing evangelicals than any other president in recent history, and he will continue to do so in his second term (see Suskind 2004: 44–51, 64, 102). What is most disturbing is not simply that many of his religious supporters believe that Bush is their leader but also that he is embraced as a "messenger from God" (Kaplan 2004), whose job it is to implement God's will. For example, Bob Jones III (2004), the president of a fundamentalist college of the same name, argued in a letter to President Bush: "Christ has allowed you to be his servant" in order to "leave an imprint for righteousness... In your re-election, God has graciously granted America – though she doesn't deserve it – a reprieve from the agenda of paganism. You have been given a mandate. We the people expect your voice to be like the clear and certain sound of a trumpet... Don't equivocate. Put your agenda on the front burner and let it boil. You owe the liberals nothing. They despise you because they despise your Christ." Jones goes on to claim that since "Christ has allowed [Bush] to be His servant in this nation ... you will have the opportunity to appoint many conservative judges and exercise forceful leadership with the Congress in passing legislation that is defined by biblical norm regarding the family, sexuality, sanctity of life, religious freedom, freedom of speech, and limited government." This is more than a call by Christian social conservatives and "power puritans," as Maureen Dowd (2004b) calls them, to appoint conservative judges, prevent homosexuals from securing jobs as teachers and approve legislation that would stop stem-cell research and eliminate the reproductive rights of women; it is also an example of the "bloodthirsty feelings of revenge" that now motivate many of Bush's religious boosters. The ideological fervor, if not call for vengeance, driving many of Bush's Christian fundamentalist supporters is also evident in the words of Bush supporter Hardy Billington who states, "To me, I just believe God controls everything, and God uses the president to keep evil down, to see the darkness and protect this nation. Other people will not protect us. God gives people choices to make. God gave us this president to be the man to protect the nation at this time" (qtd in Suskind 2004: 102). Bush seems to harbor the same arrogant illusion and out of that illusion has emerged a government that pushes aside self-criticism, uncertainty and doubt in favor of a faith-based certainty and moral righteousness bereft of critical reflection.[7] In fact, fear, slander, and God were the cornerstones of the Bush 2004 presidential campaign. First, Cheney argued that if Kerry were elected, his election would mean the country would be subjected to terrorists attacks, which amounted to "Vote Bush or Die." Second, the Swift Boat campaign successfully led the American people to believe that Kerry was a coward rather than a war hero, in spite of the five medals he won in Vietnam. And, finally, God became the ultimate referent to mobilize millions of additional votes from Christian fundamentalists. Matthew Rothschild (2004: 4), the editor of *The Progressive*, points out that the Republicans sent out pieces of literature in Arkansas and West Virginia "claiming the Democrats were going to take everyone's Bibles away... On the front of one such envelope, sent from the Republican National Committee, was a picture of a Bible with the word 'BANNED' slapped across it. 'This will be Arkansas ... if you don't vote,' it said." It appears that the high-pitched righteousness proclaimed by Bush's evangelical army of supporters took a vacation in order to play dirty politics during the Bush/Kerry campaign.

Ron Suskind (2004: 47) has argued that the one key feature of Bush's faith-based presidency is that it scorns "open dialogue, based on facts, [which] is not seen as something of inherent value." Jim Wallis, a progressive evangelical pastor who was called upon by Bush to bring together a range of clergy to talk about faith and poverty, discovered rather quickly that the president was not open to inconvenient facts or ideas at odds with what Bush often refers to as "his instincts." Wallis claims that as he got to work over time with Bush in the White House what he "started to see at this point was that man that would emerge over the next year – a messianic American Calvinist. He doesn't want to hear from anyone who doubts him" (qtd in Suskind 2004: 50). Bush became widely recognized as a president that exhibited a dislike, if not disdain, for contemplation, examining the facts, and dealing with friendly queries about the reasons for his decisions. Rampant anti-intellectualism coupled with Taliban-like moralism now boldly translates into everyday cultural practices as right-wing evangelicals live out their messianic view of the world. For instance, more and more conservative pharmacists are refusing to fill prescriptions for religious reasons. Mixing medicine, politics and religion means that some women are being denied birth-control pills or any other product designed to prevent conception. It gets worse. Bush's much-exalted religious fundamentalism does more than promote a disdain for critical thought and reinforce retrograde forms of homophobia and patriarchy; it also inspires an aggressive militarism, wrapped up in the language of a holy war. *Agence France Presse* (2004) reported that a group of evangelical marines prepared to "battle barbarians" before their assault on Fallujah in Iraq by listening to heavy metal-flavored lyrics in praise of Christ while a "female voice cried out on the loudspeakers 'You are the sovereign, Your name is holy. You are the pure spotless lamb.'" Just before the battle, a chaplain had the soldiers line up in order to dab their heads with oil, while he told them "God's people would be anointed with oil." It now appears that Bush's war for "democracy" is defined by many of his followers as a "holy war" against infidels.

The third antidemocratic dogma is visible in the relentless attempt on the part of the Bush administration to destroy critical education as a foundation for an engaged citizenry and a vibrant democracy. The attack on critical education is evident not only in the attempt to standardize curricula, privatize public schooling, and use the language of business as a model for running schools, but also in the ongoing effort to hand over those larger educational forces in the culture to a small group of corporate interests. Schooling is reduced to training, rote learning and, with regard to poor minorities in poverty stricken neighborhoods, becomes a form of warehousing. Teachers are now viewed as either technicians, depoliticized professionals, or if they belong to a teachers' union, as former Education Secretary Rod Paige pointed out, as members of a "terrorist organization" (qtd in King 2004).

At the same time as democracy is removed from the purpose and meaning of schooling, the dominant media are increasingly reduced to propaganda machines, available to the highest corporate bidder. As is commonly known, the major media outlets in the United States are controlled by six companies and the six largest cable companies reach 80 percent of cable television subscribers (see Bagdikian 2004). Under the Bush administration, deregulation intensifies such concentration and further undermines any possibility of an independent and critical media. For instance, three firms in the largest radio market now control access to more than half of the listening audience. One of the firms, Clear Channel Communications, owns 1,225 stations in the United States "and reaches ... more than 70 percent of the American public" (Sharlet 2003: 38–9). Under such circumstances, democracy is hijacked by private interests and the marketplace of ideas has almost nothing to do with providing citizens with knowledge that is crucial in order to be active participants in shaping and sustaining a vibrant democracy. On the contrary, the media largely serves to target audiences for advertising, to pander to the antiliberal ideologies of the political elite, to function in large part to reinforce the conventional wisdom of corporate interests, and to help produce a populace absorbed in cynical withdrawal and adrift in a sea of celebrity scandal and mindless infotainment and militainment. Under the sway of a market fundamentalism, the dominant media have deteriorated into a combination of commercialism, propaganda and entertainment.[8] Under such circumstances, the media neither operates in the interests of the public good nor provides the pedagogical conditions necessary for producing critical citizens or defending a vibrant democracy. Instead, as McChesney and Nichols

(2002: 52–3) point out, concentrated media depoliticizes the culture of politics, carpet bombs its citizens commercially and denigrates public life. Rather than perform an essential public service, it has become the primary tool for promoting a culture of consent and conformity in which citizens are misinformed and public discourse is debased. Media concentration restricts the range of views to which people have access and in doing so does a disservice to democracy itself. For example, *NOW with Bill Moyers* (2004: 2) did a radio survey in which it was discovered that "the top-rated talk radio stations across the country ran 310 hours of conservative talk each day and only five hours of views that were not right-wing." But the dominant media do more than peddle conservative ideologies and turn citizens into panting consumers; they also cheapen political discourse if not intelligence itself. How else to explain *The Village Voice* columnist Rick Perlstein's revelation that when he asked a number of political shakers and movers from the Democratic party about how the Bush administration was stealing Americans' democratic birthright, he was told that he was proposing an "elite argument"? Jeff Shesol, a former speech writer for President Clinton exemplifies how the discourse about democracy and politics has been cheapened. According to Shesol, any attempt to talk critically about the future of democracy to a larger public is unproductive because, "It pitches too high to reach the mass electorate" (qtd in Perlstein 2004).

According to Perlstein, highly placed Democratic party operatives believe that arguments that focus on the fragility or highjacking of democracy are now considered too abstract for public consumption. Surely, this suggests an educational as well as a moral failing. Hence, it is not too far-fetched to argue that education as schooling or as public pedagogy now generally functions "to limit the instruments for complex and critical reasoning" (Eco 1995: 15). Under the Bush administration, especially in its move to create a national security state, diverse pedagogical modes of address and sites of education are increasingly being appropriated in an effort to diminish the capacity of the American public to think critically. As the critical power of education both within and outside institutional schooling is reduced to the official discourse of compliance, conformity and reverence, it becomes more difficult for the American public to engage in critical debates, translate private considerations into public concerns and recognize the distortions and lies that underlie much of current government policy. How else to explain how Bush was reelected in 2004 in the face of flagrant lies about why the US invaded Iraq, the passing of tax reform policies that reward the ultrarich at the expense of the middle and lower classes, and the pushing of a foreign policy platform that the rest of the world largely equates with bullying? What is one to make of Bush's winning popular support for his reelection in light of his record of letting millions of young people slide into poverty and hopelessness, his continued "assault on regulations designed to protect public health and the environment" and his promulgation of a culture of fear that is gutting the most cherished of American civil liberties?[9]

Finally, another antidemocratic dogma that is shaping American life, and one of the most disturbing, is the ongoing militarization of public life. Such a doctrine not only shapes a foreign policy that ignores multilateral cooperation with other nations, but it is also based on a policy of preemptive strikes "that posits military might as a salvific in a world in which he who has the most and biggest weapons is the more moral and masculine, hence worthy of policing others" (West 2004: 5). But as Cornel West also points out, such aggressive militarism is fashioned out of an ideology that not only supports a foreign policy based on "the cowboy mythology of the American frontier fantasy," but also affects domestic policy because it expands "police power, augments the prison-industrial complex, and legitimates unchecked male power (and violence) at home and in the workplace. It views crime as a monstrous enemy to crush (targeting poor people) rather than as an ugly behavior to change (by addressing the conditions that often encourage such behavior)" (ibid.: 6).

As the politics of fear undermines any feasible attempt to reclaim democratic values conducive to producing and legitimating shared civic responsibilities, the ideology of war and the militarization of public life both legitimate the rise of the military-industrial-prison-educational-entertainment complex and put into play forms of masculinity in which aggression, violence and a hyped-up bravado set the tone for what it means to be a "real" man in America. Within this climate of degraded masculinity, Governor Arnold Schwarzenegger is entirely untroubled using the term "girlie men" to disparage his allegedly liberal counterparts in California who called attention to the consequences of Bush's economic doctrine. Nor is the military unsettled about producing video games, such as *America's Army*, which link masculinity to killing and hunting "foreign" enemies and which are distributed primarily as recruiting tools to get young men and women to join in the "adventure" taking place in Iraq and Afghanistan. The US army's *America's Army* is distributed as a free CD-ROM and is also free to use on many gaming websites. The video game has become so popular that the army staged a tournament in New York and had recruiters waiting at the door (Thompson 2004). Furthermore, the army purchased and maintains its own video game production studio.

As the military becomes more popular in American life, its under-lying values, social relations, ideology and hypermasculine esthetic begin to spread out into other aspects of American culture. Citizens are recruited as foot soldiers in the war on terrorism, urged to spy on their neighbors' behaviors, watch for suspicious-looking people and supply data to government sources in the war on terrorism. As permanent war becomes a staple of everyday life, flags appear everywhere as a show of support for both the expanding interests of empire abroad and the increasing militarization of the culture and social order at home. Major universities now compete for defense contracts and rush to build courses and programs that cater to the interests of the Department of Homeland Security. Congress recently passed legislation that would "stiffen penalties for colleges that bar military recruiters from their campuses" (Field 2004). Public schools not only have more military recruiters, but they also have more military personnel teaching in the classrooms.

Schools were once viewed as democratic public spheres that would teach students how to resist the militarization of democratic life, or at least learn the skills to peacefully engage domestic and international problems. Now they serve as recruiting stations for students to fight colonizing wars abroad. In addition, schools now adopt the logic of tough love by implementing zero-tolerance policies that effectively model urban public schools after prisons, just as students' rights continue to diminish under the onslaught of a military-style discipline. Students in many schools, especially those in poor urban areas, are routinely searched, frisked, subjected to involuntary drug tests, maced and carted off to jail. The not-so-hidden curriculum here is that kids can't be trusted and that their rights are not worth protecting. At the same time, students are being educated to passively accept military-sanctioned practices organized around maintaining control, surveillance and unquestioned authority, all conditions central to a police state and protofascism. But children and schools are not the only victims of a growing militarization of American society. The civil rights of people of color and immigrants, especially Arabs and Muslims, are being violated, often resulting in either imprisonment, deportment, or government harassment. Similarly, black and brown youths and adults are being incarcerated at record levels as prison construction outstrips the construction of schools, hospitals and other life-preserving institutions. In California, beginning correctional officers earn more than the average public school teacher. All this is happening in the name of antiterrorism laws that are increasingly also being used by the Bush administration to justify abusive military campaigns abroad and to stifle dissent at home.

Measures to combat terrorism are now used by the government to support an arms budget that is larger than those of all other major industrialized countries combined. As the state increasingly functions largely in its capacity to expand the forces of domestic militarization, surveillance, and control, it appears that the Bush administration is waging a war against democracy itself. Militarism has become a new public pedagogy, and one of its consequences is a growing authoritarianism that encourages profit-hungry monopolies, the ideology of faith-based certainty and the undermining of any vestige of critical education, dissent, and dialog. Education either is severely narrowed and trivialized in the media or is converted into training and character reform in the schools. Within higher education, democracy appears as an excess, if not a pathology, as right-wing ideologues and corporate wannabe administrators increasingly police what faculty say, teach, and do in their courses. And it is going to get worse.

THE PROMISE OF PEDAGOGY, CULTURAL POLITICS AND EDUCATED HOPE

If George W. Bush's first term appeared as an aberration due to "an electoral quirk, the fruit of a Florida Fiasco, the arcane algebra of the US electoral system, and a split decision of the supreme court" (Freedland 2004), it now appears that his reelection in 2004 is a dangerous turning point in American history. Not only did he receive slightly more than 50 percent of the popular vote, but he also garnered a mandate for a mode of leadership and set of domestic and foreign policies that bring the United States close to the edge of a totalitarian regime. George W. Bush's reelection is tantamount to a revolution aimed at rolling back most of the democratic gains of the last century. Paul Krugman is right in arguing that "Bush isn't a conservative. He's a radical – the leader of a coalition that deeply dislikes America as it is. Part of that coalition wants to tear down the legacy of Franklin Roosevelt, eviscerating Social Security and, eventually, Medicare. Another part wants to break down the barriers between church and state" (2004: A27). Under Bush's first term as president, growing appeals to fear and insecurity coupled with a growing militarism, authoritarianism and culture of cynicism became the most powerful values and forces shaping public life. Hence, it is not surprising that Karl Rove, Bush's chief strategist, most admires the Gilded Age under the presidency of William McKinley (1896–1901), a period when robber barons and strikebreakers ruled and the government and economy were controlled by a cabal that was rich, powerful, and ruthless. Given that Bush's campaign was run by "dividing the country along [the] fault lines of fear, intolerance, ignorance and religious rule" (Dowd 2004a: A27), the future does not look bright for democracy. Critical race theorist David Theo Goldberg got it right in arguing that the message of the election is:

> don't get ill, lose your job, or retire; don't breathe, swim in the ocean, travel, or think critical thoughts; invest your life-savings in the stock market even though you will likely lose it all; go to community college for two years of technical training rather than to four-year universities where your mind will be turned to liberal mush; support tax cuts for the wealthy, and military service for the poor. If you step out of line, remember the Patriot Act is there to police you at home and a loaded B52 bomber hovers overhead abroad. (2004: 3)

In opposition to this deeply reactionary revolution being waged by political extremists, Christian fundamentalists and free-market evangelicals, composition theorists, critical educators, artists, and other cultural workers need to try to connect to the energies of a deep democratic tradition extending from Horace Mann to W.E.B. DuBois to John Dewey. Such a critical tradition is both moving and theoretically useful because it not only examines the long legacy of the struggle for democracy in the schools, but also argues for struggling over public and higher education as one of the few public spaces left where democracy can actually be taught, experienced, and defended. Educators, students, and others need to make clear that education and politics as they are being practiced in Washington DC are no longer about democracy, the public good, public participation, or critical citizenship. What needs to be recognized is that under the auspices of a diverse group of extremists, including political, religious, and market fundamentalists, political and educational culture is being transformed into the discourse of privatization, consumerism, market-based choice, the spectacle of celebrity and the revived ethics of social Darwinism. Abstracted from the ideal of public commitment, the new authoritarianism represents a political and economic practice and form of militarism that loosens the connection between substantive democracy, critical agency, and critical education.

Against this rising tide of authoritarianism, educators must make a case for linking learning to social change, pluralizing and critically engaging the diverse sites where public pedagogy takes place. They must also make clear that every sphere of social life is open to political contestation and constitutes a crucial site of political, social and cultural struggle in the attempt to forge the knowledge, identifications, affective investments and social relations that constitute a political subject and social agent capable of energizing and spreading the basis of a global radical democracy. Educators need to develop a new discourse as part of a broader, sustained attempt to develop a democratic politics and pedagogy that combine the legacy of social justice, equality, freedom and rights associated with the democratic concerns of history, space, plurality, power, discourse, identities, morality, and the future.

Under such circumstances, pedagogy must be embraced as a moral and political practice, one that is both directive and the outgrowth of struggles designed to resist the increasing depoliticization of political culture that is the hallmark of the current Bush revolution. Education is the terrain where consciousness is shaped, needs are constructed, and the capacity for self-reflection and social change is nurtured and produced. Education has assumed an unparalleled significance in shaping the language, values, and ideologies that legitimate the structures and organizations that support the imperatives of global capitalism. Rather than being simply a technique or methodology, education has become a crucial site for the production of and struggle over those pedagogical and political conditions that allow people to believe it is possible to develop forms of agency that enable them to intervene individually and collectively in the processes through which the material relations of power shape the meaning and practices of their everyday lives. Within the current historical context, struggles over power take on a symbolic and discursive as well as a material and institutional form. The struggle over education is about more than the struggle over meaning and identity; it is also about how meaning, knowledge and values are produced, legitimated, and operate within economic and structural relations of power.

Education is not at odds with politics; it is an important element in any definition of the concept of the political and offers not only the theoretical tools for a systemic critique of authoritarianism, but also a language of possibility for creating actual movements for democratic social change. At stake here is combining an interest in symbolic forms and processes conducive to democratization with broader social contexts and the institutional formations of power itself. The key point here is to understand and engage pedagogical practices from the point of view of how they are bound up with larger relations of power. Educators, students, and parents need to be clearer about how power works through and in texts, representations, and discourses while at the same time recognizing that power cannot be limited to the study of representations and discourses. Changing consciousness is not the same as altering the institutional basis of oppression, but at the same time institutional reform cannot take place without a change in consciousness capable of recognizing the very need for such change or the need to reinvent the conditions and practices that make it possible. In addition, it is crucial to raise questions about the relationship between pedagogy and civic culture on the one hand, and what it takes for individuals and social groups to believe that they have any responsibility whatsoever to even address the realities of class, race, gender and other specific forms of domination on the other. For too long the left has ignored that the issue of politics as a strategy is inextricably connected to the issue of political education and to what it means to acknowledge that education is always tangled up with power, ideologies, values, and the acquisition of both particular forms of agency and specific visions of the future.

If public and higher education are crucial spheres for producing citizens equipped to exercise their freedoms and competent to question the basic assumptions that govern democratic political life, teachers in both public schools and higher education will have to assume their responsibility as citizen-scholars by taking critical positions; relating their work to larger social issues; offering students knowledge, debate, and dialogue about pressing social problems; and providing the conditions for students to have hope and believe that civic life matters and that they *can* make a difference in shaping it so as to expand its democratic possibilities for all groups. This suggests that educators need to take positions without standing still and make available those ideas, values and theories that can critically challenge official knowledge that indiscriminately embraces both religious fundamentalism and neoliberal ideology. Educators now face the daunting challenge of creating new discourses, pedagogies and collective strategies that will offer students the hope and tools necessary to revive the culture of politics as an ethical response to the demise of democratic public life. Such a challenge suggests struggling to keep alive those institutional spaces, forums, and public spheres that support and defend critical education; helping students come to terms with their own power as individual and social agents; exercising civic courage and engaging in community projects and research that are socially responsible, while refusing to surrender knowledge and skills to the highest bidder. In part, this requires pedagogical practices that connect the production of language, culture and identity to their deployment in larger physical and social spaces. Such a pedagogy is based on the presupposition that it is not enough to teach students to break with accepted ideas. They must also learn to confront directly the threats from fundamentalisms of all varieties that seek to turn democracy into a mall, a sectarian church, or a wing of the coming carceral state – a set of options that must be understood as an assault on democracy.

There are those critics who in tough economic times insist that providing students with anything other than work skills threatens their future viability on the job market. While I believe that education should equip students with skills to enter the workplace, it should also educate them to contest workplace inequalities, imagine democratically organized forms of work, and identify and challenge those injustices that contradict and undercut the most fundamental principles of freedom, equality and respect for all people who constitute the global public sphere. Public and higher education are about more than job preparation or even critical consciousness-raising; they are also about imagining different futures and politics as a form of intervention into public life. In contrast to the cynicism and political withdrawal that media culture fosters, a critical education demands that its citizens be able to translate the interface of private considerations and public issues; be able to recognize those antidemocratic forces that deny social, economic and political justice; and be willing to give some thought to their experiences as a matter of anticipating and struggling for a better world. In short, democratic rather than commercial values should be the primary concerns of both public education and the university.

If right-wing reforms in public and higher education continue unchallenged, the consequences will reflect a society in which a highly trained, largely white elite will take command of the techno-information revolution while a vast, low-skilled majority of poor and minority workers will be relegated to competing with their grandparents to fill the McJobs proliferating in the service sector. In contrast to this vision, it is important that genuine, critical education not be confused with job training. If educators and others are to prevent this distinction from becoming blurred, it is crucial for them both to challenge the ongoing corporatization of public schools and higher education and to uphold the promise of the modern social contract in which all youth is guaranteed the necessary protections and opportunities, and is viewed as a primary source of economic and moral investment, and symbolizes the hope for a democratic future. In short, educators need to recapture their commitment to future generations by taking seriously the Protestant theologian Dietrich Bonhoeffer's belief that the ultimate test of morality for any democratic society resides in the condition of its children. If public and higher education are to honor this ethical commitment, they will not only have to reestablish their obligation to young people, but also reclaim their role as democratic public spheres.

In an age when schooling is reduced to training and excessive testing, and public and higher education are leasing themselves out to the highest corporate bidders, it becomes all the more imperative to view schooling and pedagogy as part of a broader democratic project to provide students with the knowledge, skills and resources they need to view themselves as critical citizens who can actively participate in understanding and shaping the forces that govern their lives. We must be reminded that education is wedded to an inherently utopian project, one that encourages students and others to reconceptualize themselves as critical social agents able to imagine a world beyond the one they know while struggling to enable the forms and institutions central to a healthy democratic culture and social order.

Unlike some theorists who suggest that politics as a site of contestation, critical exchange and engagement has either come to an end or is in a state of terminal arrest, I believe that the current depressing state of politics points to the urgent challenge of reformulating the crises of democracy as part of the fundamental crisis of vision, meaning, education, and political agency. Politics devoid of vision degenerates into either cynicism or appropriates a view of power equated with domination. Lost from such accounts is the recognition that democracy has to be struggled over – even in the face of a most appalling crisis of educational opportunity and political agency. There is also too little attention paid to the fact that the struggle over politics and democracy is inextricably linked to creating and sustaining public spheres where individuals can be educated to perform as political agents equipped with the skills, capacities and knowledge they need not only to actually perform as autonomous political agents but also to believe that such struggles are worth taking up. It also means taking back people's time in an era when the majority must work more than they ever have to make ends meet. The struggle over time is not merely a work issue; it is also about creating the conditions in which time becomes an asset rather than a liability and offers individuals the opportunity to actually be involved in those deliberative processes and actions that give public life substantive meaning. Jo Ellen Green Kaiser is right in arguing that American culture not only lacks the public spaces in which democracy can flourish, but it also "lacks the time for democracy to grow and flourish" (2003: 17–18). The growth of cynicism in American society might say less about the reputed apathy of the populace than it says about the bankruptcy of the old political languages and the need for a new language and vision for clarifying intellectual, ethical, and political projects, especially as they work to reframe questions of agency, ethics and meaning for a substantive democracy.

Yet crafting a new political language requires what I call educated hope. Hope, in this instance, is the precondition for individual and social struggle, involving the ongoing practice of critical education in a wide variety of sites and the renewal of civic courage among citizens who wish to address pressing social problems. In this sense, educated hope is a subversive force. In opposition to those who seek to turn hope into a new slogan or punish and dismiss efforts to look beyond the horizon of the given, educators need to resurrect a language of resistance and possibility, a language in which hope is viewed as both a project and a pedagogical condition for providing a sense of opposition and engaged struggle. As a project, Andrew Benjamin insists hope must be viewed as "a structural condition of the present rather than as the promise of a future, the continual promise of a future that will always have to have been better" (1997: 1). Rather than viewed as an individual proclivity, hope is essential to any educational project aligned with the promise of democracy and must be seen as part of a broader politics that acknowledges those social, economic, spiritual, and cultural conditions in the present that make certain kinds of agency and democratic politics possible. In this instance, hope becomes anticipatory rather than messianic, mobilizing rather than therapeutic. The longing for a more humane society does not collapse into a retreat from the world but emerges out of critical and practical engagements with present behaviors, institutional formations and everyday practices. Hope in this context does not ignore the worst dimensions of human suffering, exploitation and social relations; on the contrary, it acknowledges the need to sustain the "capacity to see the worst and offer more than that for our consideration" (Dunn 2000: 160).

Hence, hope is more than a politics; it is also a pedagogical and performative practice that provides the foundation for enabling human beings to learn about their potential as moral and civic agents. Hope is the outcome of those pedagogical practices and struggles that tap into memory and lived experiences while at the same time linking individual responsibility with a progressive sense of social change. As a form of utopian longing, educated hope opens up horizons of comparison by evoking not just different histories but also different futures; at the same time, it substantiates the importance of ambivalence while problematizing certainty or, as Paul Ricoeur has suggested, it serves as "a major resource as the weapon against closure" (qtd in Bauman 1998: 98). Educated hope is a subversive force when it pluralizes politics by opening up a space for dissent, makes authority accountable and becomes an activating presence in promoting social transformation.

The current limits of the utopian imagination, especially in light of the reelection of George W. Bush, are related, in part, to the failure of many educators and others to imagine what pedagogical conditions might be necessary to bring into being forms of political agency that might expand the operations of individual rights, social justice, and democratic freedoms. At the same time, a politics and pedagogy of hope is neither a blueprint for the future nor a form of social engineering, but a belief, simply, that different futures are possible, holding open matters of contingency, context and indeterminacy. It is only through critical forms of education that human beings can learn about the limits of the present and the conditions necessary for them to "combine a gritty sense of limits with a lofty vision of possibility" (Aronson 1999: 489). Hope as both an ethical referent and a performative practice poses the important challenge of how to reclaim social agency within a broader struggle to deepen the possibilities for social justice and global democracy. This position is echoed by Judith Butler, who argues, "For me there is more hope in the world when we can question what is taken for granted, especially about what it is to be human" (qtd in Olson and Worsham 2000: 765). Any educational project informed by the promise of a critical and inclusive democracy must recognize that the resurrection of any viable notion of political and social agency is dependent upon a culture of questioning, the purpose of which is to "keep the forever unexhausted and unfulfilled human potential open, fighting back all attempts to foreclose and pre-empt the further unraveling of human possibilities, prodding human society to go on questioning itself and preventing that questioning from ever stalling or being declared finished" (Bauman and Tester 2001: 4).

Coupling education and democracy rests on the assumption that pedagogy plays a crucial role in creating the conditions, knowledge and skills that allow people to embrace hope rather than cynicism, to be responsible to themselves and others rather than surrender their sense of agency to either corporations or authoritarian despots, to take an essential step toward self-representation rather than mimicking the dictates of a consumer culture, to act from a position of critical agency rather than from a position of subservience, and to break through the modes of alienation that tie them to the "commonsense" of neoliberalism and the new global order. In this sense, pedagogy becomes less a manifesto proclaiming a fixed politics than a form of mediation, an intervention, that attempts to connect educators and other activists to old and new locations of struggle in an attempt to deepen and broaden both the reality and the possibilities of democratic public life. This suggests modes of critical education that attempt to come to grips with the changing conditions of politics, while at the same time offering educators a language of critique and possibility for becoming public intellectuals capable of linking education to critical agency, and public and higher education to broader public considerations and social issues.

All this may seem hopelessly romantic, operating largely in the realm of fantasy, but it is crucial to realize, as the journalist Bill Moyers (2003) has argued in a different context, that education and "democracy are deeply linked in whatever chance we human beings have to redress our grievances, renew our politics, and reclaim our revolutionary ideals. Those are difficult tasks at any time, and they are even more difficult in a cynical age as this, when a deep and pervasive corruption has settled upon the republic." Of course, too much is at stake for educators and others to ignore this battle over making education a central foundation for a substantive democracy. Rather than retreating into either cynicism or despair, educators need to find new ways to use theory as a resource to rethink the meaning of democracy, the role of educators as public intellectuals and what it might mean in an age of increasing antidemocratic dogmas and an unchecked market authoritarianism to reconsider the nature of politics and forms of intervention that can combine education with a new democratic project infused with a sense of social justice and a strong hostility to the existence of human suffering and exploitation.

NOTES

I want to thank Grace Pollock, Jake Kennedy and Christopher Robbins, my research assistants, for their invaluable help with this article.

1. Cited from the transcript: "Elizabeth Farnsworth reports on President-elect George W. Bush's first day in Washington," *OnLine News Hour With Jim Lehrer* (December 18, 2000). Available online: http://www.pbs.org/newshour/bb/politics/July-dec00/trans_12-18.htm.
2. For a brilliant analysis of the Bush administration policies after the events of September 11th, see Street 2004.
3. I take up this issue in Giroux 2004a. For a history of free speech under attack in the United States, see Stone 2004.
4. On the fiscal irresponsibility of the Bush administration and the politics of the debt limit, see Gross 2004.
5. I have taken up the growing authoritarianism in American life in Giroux 2004b.
6. What now seems a typical occurrence is the takeover of school boards by right-wing Christian fundamentalists who then impose the teaching of creationism on the schools. See, for example, Associated Press 2004b, "Wisconsin School OKs Creationism Teaching." For a more extensive analysis of the right-wing social conservative attack on modernity, science and reason, see Heuvel 2004.
7. One of the most frightening examples of this arrogance of power and easy certainty can be seen in an exchange Ron Suskind had

with one of Bush's aides. He writes: "The aide said that guys like me were 'in what we call the reality-based community,' which he defined as people who 'believe that solutions emerge from your judicious study of discernible reality.' I nodded and murmured something about enlightenment principles and empiricism. He cut me off. 'That is not the way the world really works anymore,' he continued. 'We're an empire now, and when we act, we create our own reality. And while you're studying that reality – judiciously, as you will – we'll act again, creating other new realities, which you can study too, and that's how things will sort out. We're history's actors … and you, all of you, will be left to just study what we do'" (2004: 51). This is not so much a matter of faith producing a blinding arrogance as it is a fundamentalism that not only sees democracy as the enemy, but also prepares the groundwork for a faith-based authoritarianism or a new form of fascism.

8. On the relationship between democracy and the media, see McChesney 1999.

9. Paul O'Neill, former Treasury Secretary who served in the Bush administration for two years, claimed on the January 11, 2004 television program *60 Minutes* that Bush and his advisers started talking about invading Iraq ten days after the inauguration, eight months before the tragic events of September 11th. See CBS News 2004. For a chronicle of lies coming out of the Bush administration, see Corn 2003. On the environment, see Borenstein 2004.

REFERENCES

Agence France Presse News Line. 2004. "Holy War: Evangelical Marines Prepare to Battle Barbarians." *Common Dreams News Center* (November 7). Available online: http://www.commondreams.org/headlines04/1107–02.htm.

Aronson, Ron. 1999. "Hope After Hope?" *Social Research* 66(2): 471–9.

Associated Press. 2004a. "Scientists Group Says Bush Administration Ignores, Distorts Research." *The Sun Herald* (February 18). Available online: http://www.sunherald.com/mld/sunherald/business/technology/7982691.htm 18feb04.

—— 2004b. "Wisconsin School OKs Creationism Teaching." *Common Dreams News Center* (November 6). Available online: http://www.commondreams.org/headlines04/1106–08.htm.

Bagdikian, Ben H. 2004. *The New Media Monopoly.* Boston: Beacon Press.

Bauman, Zygmunt. 1998. *Work, Consumerism and the New Poor.* Philadelphia: Open University Press.

—— 2001. *The Individualized Society.* London: Polity Press.

Bauman, Zygmunt and Tester, Keith. 2001. *Conversations with Zygmunt Bauman.* Malden: Polity Press.

CBS News. 2004. "Bush Sought Way to Invade Iraq." *60 Minutes* transcript (July 11). Available online: http://www.cbsnews.com/stories/2004/01/09/60minutes/main592330.shtml.

Benjamin, Andrew. 1997. *Present Hope: Philosophy, Architecture, Judaism*. New York: Routledge.

Borenstein, Seth. 2004. "Environment Worsened Under Bush in Many Key Areas, Data Show." *Common Dreams News Center* (October 13). Available online: www.commondreams.org/headlines04/1013–12.htm.

Claxton, Melvin and Hansen, Ronald J. 2004. "Working Poor Suffer Under Bush Tax Cuts." *The Detroit News* (September 26). Available online: www.detnews.com/2004/specialreport/0409/26/a01-284666.

Connolly, Cece and Wittem, Griff. 2004. "Poverty Rate Up 3rd Year In a Row." *The Washington Post* (August 27), p. A1.

Corn, David. 2003. *The Lies of George Bush*. New York: Crown.

Dowd, Maureen. 2004a. "The Red Zone." *New York Times* (November 4), p. A27.

—— 2004b. "Slapping the Other Cheek." *New York Times* (November 14). Available online: http://www.nytimes.com/2004/11/14/opinion/14dowd.html?oref=login&hp.

Dunn, Thomas L. 2000. "Political Theory for Losers." In Jason A. Frank and John Tambornino (eds), *Vocations of Political Theory*. Minneapolis: University of Minnesota Press, pp. 145–65.

Eakin, Hugh. 2004. "Just Like in the Movies." *New York Times Book Review* (November 7), p. 9.

Eco, Umberto. 1995. "Eternal Fascism: Fourteen Ways of Looking at a Blackshirt." *The New York Review of Books* (November–December), pp. 12–15.

Feldman, Allen. 2004. "Abu Ghraib: Ceremonies of Nostalgia." *Open Democracy* (October 18), p. 1–3.

Field, Kelly. 2004. "Colleges That Ban Military Recruiters Would Lose Additional Funds Under New Legislation." *The Chronicle of Higher Education* (October 11). Available online: http://chronicle.com/prm/weekly/v51/i16/16a00101.htm.

Freedland, Jonathan. 2004. "This is no Passing Phase. This is now an Era." *The Guardian* (November 4). Available online: http://www.guardian.co.uk/print/0,3858,5054801-112564,00.html.

Giroux, Henry A. 2004a. *The Abandoned Generation: Democracy Beyond The Culture of Fear*. New York: Palgrave.

Giroux, Henry A. and Searls Giroux, Susan. 2004. *Take Back Higher Education: Race, Youth, and the Crisis of Democracy in the Post Civil Rights Era*. New York: Palgrave.

—— 2004b. *The Terror of Neoliberalism: Authoritarianism and the Eclipse of Democracy*. Boulder: Paradigm Press.

Goldberg, David Theo. 2004. "The Sovereign's Smirk." *Open Democracy* (November 3), p. 3.

Greider, William. 2003. "The Right's Grand Ambition: Rolling Back the 20th Century." *The Nation* (May 12), pp. 1–12.

—— 2004. "Under the Banner of the 'War' on Terror." *The Nation* (June 21), pp. 11–18.

CULTURAL POLITICS

Gross, Daniel. 2004. "Why Democrats Should be Thankful: At Least They Don't Have to Clean Up the Bush Fiscal Catastrophe." *Slate* (November 4). Available online: http://slate.msn.com/id/2109203/#ContinueArticle.

Heuvel, Katrina vanden. 2004. "Creeping Creationism." *Common Dreams News Center* (November 22). Available online: www.commondreams.org/views04/1120-21.htm.

Hitchens, Christopher. 2004. "War of Words." *New York Times Book Review* (November 7), pp. 8–9.

Holt, Jim. 2004. "The Other National Conversation." *New York Times Sunday Magazine* (November 7), p. 17.

Hopkins, Andrea. 2004. "Nearly 36 Million Americans Living in Poverty." *Common Dreams News Center* (August 26). Available online: www.commondreams.org/headlines04/0826-24.htm.

Ivins, Molly. 2003. "Bush Discovers Hunger and Looks the Other Way." *The Chicago Tribune* (December 26). Available online: http://flag.blackened.net/pipermail/infoshop-news/2003-February/002375.html.

Johnson, Hans. 2004. "Fiction First, Spin Later." *In These Times* (October 11), p. 20.

Jones, Bob, III. 2004. "Congratulatory Letter to President George W. Bush From Dr. Bob Jones III." Originally posted online: http://www.bju.edu/letter.

Kaiser, Jo Ellen Green. 2003. "A Politics of Time and Space." *Tikkun* 18 (6): 17–20.

Kaplan, Esther. 2004. *With God on Their Side: How Christian Fundamentalists Trampled Science, Policy and Democracy in George W. Bush's White House.* New York: The New Press.

King, John. 2004. "Paige Calls NEA a 'Terrorist Organization.'" *CNN Washington Bureau* (February 23). Available online: http://www.cnn.com/2004/EDUCATION/02/23/paige.terrorist.nea/.

Krugman, Paul. 2003. "Looting the Future." *New York Times* (December 5), p. A27.

—— 2004. "No Surrender." *New York Times* (November 5), p. A27.

McChesney, Robert W. 1999. *Rich Media, Poor Democracy: Communication Politics in Dubious Times.* New York: The New Press.

McChesney, Robert and Nichols, John. 2002. *Our Media, Not Theirs: The Democratic Struggle Against Corporate Media.* New York: Seven Stories Press.

Moyers, Bill. 2003. "Keynote Address to the National Conference on Media Reform." *Common Dreams News Center* (November 12). Available online: www.commondreams.org/views03/1112-10.htm.

NOW with Bill Moyers. 2004. Transcript (February 13).

Olson, Gary A. and Worsham, Lynn. 2000. "Changing the Subject: Judith Butler's Politics of Radical Resignification." *Journal of Composition Theory* 20(4): 727–65.

Perlstein, Rick. 2004. "The End of Democracy: Losing America's Birthright, the George Bush Way." *The Village Voice* (October 19). Available online: www.villagevoice.com/print/issues/0442/perlstein.php.

Rothschild, Matthew. 2004. "Fear, Smear, and God." *The Progressive* (November), p. 4.

Sharlet, Jeff. 2003. "Big World: How Clear Channel Programs America." *Harper's Magazine* (December), pp. 38–9.

Sklar, Holly. 2004. "Boom Time for Billionaires." *Znet Commentary* (October 12). Available online: www.zmag.org/sustainers/content/2004-10/12sklar.cfm.

Stone, Geoffrey R. 2004. *Perilous Times: Free Speech in Wartime, From the Sedition Act of 1798 to the War on Terrorism*. New York: W.W. Norton Company.

Street, Paul. 2004. *Empire and Inequality: America and the World Since 9/11*. Boulder: Paradigm Press.

Suskind, Ron. 2004. "Without a Doubt." *New York Times Magazine* (October 17), pp. 44–51, 64, 102.

Thompson, Clive. 2004. "The Making of an XBox Warrior." In *New York Times Sunday Magazine* (August 22). Available online: http://www.nytimes.com/2004/08/22/magazine/22GAMES.html?pagewanted=print&position=.

Unger, Roberto Mangabeira and West, Cornel. 1998. *The Future of American Progressivism*. Boston: Beacon Press.

Wallis, Jim. 2003. "The War on the Poor." *SojoMail* (May 7). Available online: http://www.sojo.net/index.cfm?action=sojomail.display&issue=030507.

West, Cornel. 2004. *Democracy Matters*. New York: The Penguin Press.

CULTURAL POLITICS   VOLUME 1, ISSUE 2   REPRINTS AVAILABLE   PHOTOCOPYING   © BERG 2005
                     PP 165–192   DIRECTLY FROM THE   PERMITTED BY LICENSE   PRINTED IN THE UK
                                           PUBLISHERS.   ONLY

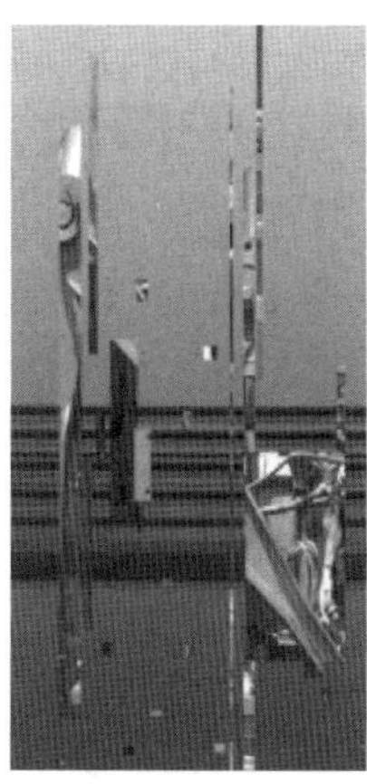

THE NEW FACE OF GLOBAL HOLLYWOOD: *BLACK HAWK DOWN* AND THE POLITICS OF META-SOVEREIGNTY

DEBBIE LISLE AND ANDREW PEPPER

DEBBIE LISLE IS A LECTURER IN POLITICS. HER RESEARCH EXAMINES THE INTERSECTIONS BETWEEN INTERNATIONAL RELATIONS AND CULTURAL STUDIES. SHE HAS PUBLISHED WORK ON WAR FILMS, TRAVEL WRITING AND TOURISM.

ANDREW PEPPER IS A LECTURER IN ENGLISH. HIS CURRENT RESEARCH EXAMINES THE HISTORY OF CRIME FICTION. HE HAS PUBLISHED WORK ON CRIME FICTION, AND REPRESENTATIONS OF AMERICAN HISTORY IN FILM.

ABSTRACT   This article uses Ridley Scott's 2001 blockbuster film *Black Hawk Down* to examine the claim that popular film is the "newest component of sovereignty." While the topic of the film – the 1993 UN/US intervention in Somalia – lends itself to straightforward politicization, this article is equally interested in the film's production history and its reception by global audiences. While initial reactions to the film focused on its ideological commitments (e.g. racism, collusion between Hollywood and the Pentagon, post-September 11th patriotism), these readings continually posed an imagined "America" against "the world." This article argues that *Black Hawk Down* is not about sovereignty as traditionally conceived, that is about national interest shaping global affairs. Rather, *Black Hawk Down* articulates, and is articulated by, a new and emerging global order that operates through inclusion, management and flexibility. Drawing on recent theoretical debates over this new logic of rule, this article illustrates how *Black Hawk Down* invokes much more diffuse, complex and deterritorialized categories than national sovereignty. In effect, Scott's film goes beyond traditional notions of sovereignty altogether: its production, signification and reception deconstruct simple notions of "America" and "the world" in favor of what Hardt and Negri call "Empire," what Zizek calls "post-politics," and what we refer to as "meta-sovereignty."

GLOBALIZATION AND THE LIMITS OF SOVEREIGN POWER

In their book *Global Hollywood,* Toby Miller et al. argue that movies are "the newest component of sovereignty, a twentieth-century cultural addition to ideas of patrimony and rights" (2001: 15). Scholars in cultural studies, film studies and international relations have analyzed how popular film reinforces both national identities (e.g. propaganda, the symbols of patriotism, national cinema movements) as well as a sense of global community (Hjort and McKenzie 2000; Lisle 2003). However, Miller et al.'s claim is different: they suggest that Hollywood film currently affects global politics *explicitly* because it has the capacity to transform the way sovereignty is both understood and practiced. This article examines Miller et al.'s argument through *Black Hawk Down*, Ridley Scott's 2001 blockbuster film that tells the story of America's UN-backed intervention in Somalia in October 1993. In doing so, it makes three principal claims; first, that efforts to understand the relationship between cinema and global politics reproduce a problematic conception of sovereignty; secondly, that a misinterpretation of sovereignty results in an inadequate understanding of how the forces of globalization – political, economic and cultural – are transforming the Hollywood film industry; and thirdly, that *Black Hawk Down* signals an opportunity to reimagine the multiple and contradictory formations of power currently at work in the global sphere.

On its initial release, the response to *Black Hawk Down* by critics, film reviewers, academics and the general public was one of intense disagreement. Many felt that the film rejuvenated American values of freedom and democracy that had been so damaged on September 11th. Others felt that this was simply another form of Hollywood propaganda used to justify a new American imperialism and secure American interests and ambitions overseas. While these two positions offer contrasting interpretations of America's presence in the world (as either benign or imperial), both reinforce the idea of an autonomous and self-determining "America" governing the global realm. And herein lies the problem: suggesting that *Black Hawk Down* represents America's benign or imperial presence on the global stage makes problematic assumptions about sovereignty. As many critical international relations scholars have argued, sovereignty is not equivalent to the nation state. Rather, it is the primary mode of authority enacted since the Early Modern period that operates according to conceptual and material discriminations such as inside/outside, citizen/alien, and domestic/international (Der Derian and Shapiro 1989; Ashley and Walker 1990; Campbell 1992; Der Derian 1992; Walker 1993; George 1994). That said, sovereignty *has* found expression in the nation state for over three centuries – and this conjunction of authority and nation is certainly Miller et al.'s understanding of sovereignty. But reading *Black Hawk Down* through this framework fails to identify how the film animates, and is animated by, a *variety* of power formations that exceed the scope of the nation state and transform the conceptual and material terrain within which sovereignty now operates. To be sure, the literature on globalization addresses some of these changes – especially the question of whether the nation state is disappearing or not – and provides an important intellectual backdrop to our concerns (Camilleri and Falk 1992; Hirst and Thompson 1996; Ohmae 1996; Mann 1997; Lisle 2005). However, we are particularly interested in recent theoretical work that illustrates how the conceptual and material legacy of sovereignty is neither disappearing nor reappearing in the form of the nation state; rather, it is being rearticulated and transformed through complex discursive networks that are diffuse, mobile and transnational.

A critical reading of Miller et al.'s argument is particularly instructive here. *Global Hollywood* certainly takes account of the forces of globalization by examining how transnational financial practices are changing the Hollywood film industry (e.g. the "liberalization" of global markets, the ever-quickening flow of capital across national boundaries, the increasingly international division of labor, and the emergence of a new breed of global managers and technocrats). Hollywood – now more than ever a shorthand term for a set of vast, interconnected, horizontally integrated entertainment mega-conglomerates – has been hugely affected by such changes, and Miller et al. are instructive about the extent to which its global reach (both in terms of production, distribution and consumption) has expanded apace throughout the 1990s. "The world," they argue, "is crucial to the US" and becoming more so. In 1998, for example, 75 percent of film tickets purchased by Western Europeans were for Hollywood films, and overseas box-office earnings ($6,821 billion) were almost equivalent to domestic earnings in America ($6,877 billion; 2001: 7, 4). Such changes raise intriguing questions about America's cultural and political position in the world – but Miller et al. are not interested in addressing the conceptual and material changes to sovereignty that underscore Hollywood's current transformations. How "American" are American films these days? To what extent are Hollywood films produced as much for audiences in Thailand as in Tennessee? And can Hollywood films affirm America's political, economic and cultural superiority while simultaneously reflecting important shifts in the way global society is organized and ruled?

With these questions in mind, we argue that Hollywood films are not simply the newest component of sovereignty, as Miller et al. claim, but rather the newest component of *meta*-sovereignty. The change is an important one. We are not suggesting that sovereignty – as a mode of authority expressed through the nation state – is an insignificant factor in the production of popular film, or in the way it commodifies and stereotypes the world for a mass audience. Our point is that an understanding of sovereignty *conceived primarily through the categories of "nation-state" and "international"* cannot explain how popular films like *Black Hawk Down* participate in a variety of global networks that exceed this categorization. We use the term meta-sovereignty to indicate the increasingly diffuse, deterritorialized and complex nature of power as it circulates in the global realm. We insist on "meta," rather than the more popular "post" as a prefix to indicate how sovereign power as expressed through the nation state is proliferating, mutating and transforming rather than disappearing. The nation state now makes use of these interconnected cultural, political, social, military and economic networks to rejuvenate itself in the face of increasing forces of globalization. For example, the World Trade Organization (WTO), as an expression of supranational political and economic authority, has not so much usurped American economic power as augmented it. In developing the term meta-sovereignty, we are by no means claiming it as an "original" category; indeed, meta-sovereignty signals a body of theoretical literature that is currently examining how sovereign power is transforming and circulating across a variety of globalized networks (Burchill et al. 1991; Hindess 1996; Campbell 1998; Shapiro 1999, 2002; Dillon and Reid 2000, 2001; Der Derian 2001; Dillon 2004; Edkins et al. 2004). Drawing on a variety of critical theorists (from Agamben to Zizek via Deleuze, Foucault and Virilio), this body of work refuses the easy generalizations of globalization (e.g. "the world is getting smaller") and insists upon a rigorous interrogation of the simultaneous conceptual and material rearticulations of power that are occurring in the global sphere. While the term meta-sovereignty both signals and draws from this body of literature, it does not indicate a coherent or seamless tradition. Indeed, there are many disagreements, contradictions and discrepancies in these approaches, and part of this paper utilizes one such debate over Michael Hardt and Antonio Negri's *Empire* to illustrate the cultural translation of meta-sovereignty in *Black Hawk Down*.

Drawing on these intellectual developments, we are primarily interested in exploring how meta-sovereignty operates in the cultural realm through popular film. It is our aim to show how a film like *Black Hawk Down* reveals slippages between the falsely opposed categories of "America" and "the world," even as American power is affirmed and rearticulated in these slippages. Certainly the world is subject to American demands in trade discussions, at the UN and in terms of military interventions – but America cannot remain unchanged by its involvement in the global realm. Nor, for that matter, can Hollywood. As such, we want to situate *Black Hawk Down* in the context of what Aida Hozic calls "Hollyworld," an imagined and all-too-real space where cinematic projections of "America" and "the world" are produced, disseminated, contested and rearticulated, and where changes in the mode of production (e.g. increased foreign investment in Hollywood, the absorption of previously autonomous film studios into giant entertainment conglomerates, the use of cheaper location shoots and film-processing plants outside the US) necessarily influence what appears on the screen (2001). Hozic forces us to think of the evolving relationship between "America" and "the world" not as mutually exclusive but, rather, as shifting, indeterminate and diffuse. In other words, she outlines a pivotal link between Hollywood and meta-sovereignty.

Reading *Black Hawk Down* in terms of its involvement in the deterritorialized, mobile and circulating relationships that are produced between "America" and "the world" requires a different methodological approach. Certainly, it is insufficient to analyze the film only at the level of the text; in other words, to argue for the film's relative merits or shortcomings only via reference to its visual grammar (e.g. how the icons, images and symbols are arranged on screen in order to produce certain connotations). While the symbolic arrangement of *Black Hawk Down* is certainly worth examining, limiting our analysis to the text itself – what appears on the screen – ignores the extent to which the mode of representation is beholden to the mode of production. In other words, particular global discourses and material constraints affect how films get produced (e.g. how they are conceived, written, financed, filmed and distributed). In addition, focusing wholly on the text overlooks the ways in which meanings, messages and connotations are constructed differently depending on who is viewing and where they are viewing from. This article shows how all three elements of *Black Hawk Down* – production, text and reception – are implicated in the powerful global transformations indicated by meta-sovereignty. This triple framework reveals that the cultural and political significance of *Black Hawk Down* does not just lie in its dialogue, music or imagery. Rather, the film's reflection of, and participation in, newly emerging patterns of global rule is also evidenced in its patterns of production and reception.

The next section outlines how complex formations of meta-sovereignty that appear in the production, text and reception of *Black Hawk Down* are ignored by popular, critical and academic responses to the film. In the months following the film's release, an intensely polarized reaction began to emerge: viewers felt that the film *either* celebrated *or* denigrated America's foreign policy. The issue here is not which interpretation is correct; rather, it is how all of the responses to *Black Hawk Down* – even the most critical ones – invoke a framework of sovereign power in which "America" and "the world" function as distinct and opposing categories. Within this framework, questions about intervention, for example, are raised and resolved only in so far as they affirm traditional understandings of how the nation state operates within an international realm. To critique this framework, the third part of the paper develops our account of meta-sovereignty by problematizing the simple relationship between "America" and "the world" through more diffuse, networked and deterritorialized formations of power. The last part then, rereads the production history, form/content and reception of *Black Hawk Down* through the concept of meta-sovereignty.

THE IDEOLOGICAL CONTAINMENT OF AMERICA

In their book *Camera Politica,* Michael Ryan and Douglas Kellner argue that the ideological power of Hollywood cinema derives from "creating an illusion that what happens on screen is a neutral recording of objective events, rather than a construct operating from a certain point of view" (1988: 1). This "certain point of view" supports existing power structures by representing itself as universal, neutral and objective and encouraging audiences to "accept the basic premises of the social order, and to ignore their irrationality and injustice" (ibid.). To read Hollywood cinema as ideology, then, requires an identification of how specific films reify unequal social relations, secure consensus to this inequality, depict this consensus as universal, and therefore uphold the agenda of those in power. In this respect, Ryan and Kellner's book is an excellent examination of how Hollywood films of the 1980s reaffirmed the conservative political orientation championed by President Reagan. But their analysis is not that simple: they are keenly aware that this "structuralist" definition of ideology "flattens out necessary distinctions between different films at different moments of history," and obscures the way that political meanings in film are "more complex, contested and differentiated" (ibid.: 1, 2). In other words, Ryan and Kellner read Hollywood film through a *critical* understanding of ideology that draws out moments of resistance to the status quo – moments that "point beyond the society of domination toward a more equal social form" (ibid.: 14).

The war film is central to this ideological framework, and Ryan and Kellner provide a useful chapter on how subversive "antiwar" films in the 1970s (e.g. *The Deer Hunter*) competed with "prowar" films of the 1980s (e.g. *Rambo II*) to overcome the "Vietnam Syndrome" (ibid.: 194–216). Because war films represent armed conflicts that "really" happened, their ideological agenda is perhaps more straightforward than in other genre films such as romantic comedies. Historically, war films have pressed this "realism" into service for ideological goals such as propaganda and recruitment (e.g. *The Green Berets*, 1968), history lessons and memorials (e.g. *Saving Private Ryan*, 1998) and even retrospective criticism (e.g. *Platoon*, 1986). However, *Black Hawk Down* does not sit easily within the tradition of Hollywood war films because it displays *contradictory* ideological messages about the intervention in Somalia: is it propaganda for American hegemony, or is it critical of America's interventionist foreign policy? Unsurprisingly, these contradictions produced an extremely polarized reception of the film from critics, academics and popular audiences. To simplify Stuart Hall's terms, audiences whose values accorded with "right-wing" political views accepted the "preferred" meaning of *Black Hawk Down* (i.e. this was an "accurate" account of the events of October 1993, which revealed the heroism and bravery of American soldiers trying to rescue starving Somalis); whereas audiences whose values accorded with "left-wing" political views drew on alternative ideological commitments and performed "oppositional" readings (i.e. this was a racist piece of propaganda that covered over the more disagreeable reasons for America's intervention in East Africa; 1993: 90–103). Despite invoking very different ideological positions (and thus supporting Ryan and Kellner's theories about the complex way ideology operates within Hollywood film), these polarized accounts share an important understanding about how a discrete "America" operates within a static international sphere. In other words, *both* readings of the film reproduce problematic and outdated assumptions about the way sovereign power currently operates in the "new world order." While we want to hold onto some of the critical points that emerge in these readings, our larger concern is how the polarized interpretations of *Black Hawk Down* fail to disrupt the notion that "America" acts – either benignly or imperially – within "the world." Rather, we are interested in showing how readings of the film from *both* positions obscure the way that Hollywood film articulates, reproduces and participates in much wider and more diffuse networks of power.

Much has been made of the rejuvenated relationship between Hollywood and the Bush administration post-September 11th 2001 – especially after Hollywood's top brass (including *Black Hawk Down* producer Jerry Bruckheimer) pledged to "commit itself to new initiatives in support of the war on terror" just a month after the attacks on New York and Washington (Walsh 2001; Carruthers 2003: 168). With *Black Hawk Down,* this rejuvenated relationship pre-dates September 11th, as the Pentagon and the Department of Defense were heavily involved in all aspects of the film's production for over a year before the Twin Towers were attacked. For both the filmmakers and the state, this relationship made practical sense. For the filmmakers, building on established links with the Pentagon and the Department of Defense meant that they struck a bargain for use of the military hardware and personnel needed to shoot the film. Only $2.2 million (out of a $90 million budget) was paid to the Pentagon for a hefty list that included two C-5 transport planes, four Black Hawk choppers, four "Little Bird" helicopters, pilots from the 160th Special Operations Aviation Regiment (SOAR), and more than 100 Army Rangers (Snead 2002). As well, the film employed three military advisers – former Navy SEAL and Vietnam Vet Harry Humphries, Lee Van Arsdale and Tom Matthews (a veteran of the 1993 Somalia mission) – who educated the production team on aspects of military protocol, Special Forces training and indoctrination (Singer 2002: 162–5; D.C. Walsh 2002). For the Pentagon and the Department of Defense, the potential benefits of such a relationship were just as self-evident. In Bruckheimer and Scott, they discovered two figures sympathetic to the project of rehabilitating the Somalian intervention as a "success" in the popular imagination. "We thought those soldiers should be remembered for their courage", Bruckheimer said, referring to an "apparent public misconception that the military messed up" in Somalia (Burlas 2002). Scott himself acknowledged the eagerness of the administration to be involved in the film: "I think the [US] army wanted this film to be made because of the misconception that it was a fiasco... From their point of view, it wasn't a fiasco. They went in there and did what they wanted to do" (Fryer 2002).

It is not difficult to see how the closeness of the Hollywood-Pentagon relationship during the production phase of *Black Hawk Down* was interpreted differently by critics – those on the right saw it as Hollywood's commendable service to the national interest, while those on the left saw it as Hollywood's lamentable capitulation to the demands of the state. Particularly revealing here was the decision to speed up the release date of the film from March 2002 to December 2001. Because this decision successfully capitalized on renewed American patriotism post-September 11th and silenced criticism in "antiwar" circles, it ensured that the "preferred" meaning of the film prevailed with audiences. In effect, the close relationship between the Pentagon and Hollywood was *normalized* in a post-11 September context: it would have been "unpatriotic" to suggest that the film's unapologetic support of American foreign policy amounted to propaganda. Instead, *Black Hawk Down* was "made-to-order mood music for the war on terror" that helped Bush mobilize support for his subsequent invasion of Afghanistan (Carruthers 2003: 168, 180).

The links between the filmmakers and the US state went beyond collaboration over practical questions of equipment and supplies, and included a shared preoccupation with the nature and content of the film's preferred message. Typical American war films set about reinforcing national myths by affirming and enabling a sense of national identity, securing a consensus for war, and promoting "noble" American soldiers on humanitarian missions abroad. As many scholars have argued, this process is easy with respect to the Second World War (the most "just" war in history), but is more difficult with any American intervention post-Vietnam – especially "Operation Restore Hope," which was perceived as a failure by the American public (Barkawi 2004; McCrisken and Pepper 2005). The filmmakers of *Black Hawk Down* had the difficult task of rewriting the intervention in Somalia as a success, and creating an "epitaph of bravery, commitment and selflessness" by honoring the nineteen American soldiers who died on the mission (Singer 2002: 152). Not surprisingly, it was the "humanitarian" angle of the film that caused the most debate – whether the American soldiers were there to rescue a starving population or further America's geopolitical ambitions. The film's opening sequence establishes the "preferred meaning" of the humanitarian angle very clearly: in typeface, we are given a sequence of "facts": (a) that the famine has been *caused* by warring clans, (b) that behind a force of 100,000 US Marines, food was delivered and order restored, (c) that Mohamed Farrah Aidid destroys that order by declaring war on the UN and US peacekeepers, and (d) that Aidid's actions precipitate the intervention of more US troops, notably the "elite" Delta Force and Army Rangers. This "factual" information is delivered over stereotypical images of Africa now familiar to Western audiences – emaciated black bodies, deserted villages, aid workers feeding the starving, the wretched and destitute dying in makeshift hospitals. In short, these people have to be *rescued.* To reinforce this message, the first scene after the title sequence is a Red Cross food distribution center under attack from Aidid – a scene in which the idealistic hero of the film, Sgt Eversmann, played by Josh Hartnett, is introduced. Circling in a Black Hawk helicopter, Eversmann is horrified that the militia are firing on unarmed civilians – but the American soldiers are helpless in the face of the atrocity because the UN mandate prevents them from engaging unless they are fired upon directly.

Both the "factual" explanations and the food distribution scene lay all blame for the crisis on the Somali warlords, particularly Aidid, but they also secure the position of the US/UN forces as heroic rescuers. By framing the conflict in these terms, the *rightness* of the intervention in Somalia is unquestioned from the outset. As Scott himself explains:

> In the end are the obvious questions about whether or not the United States had a right to be in Somalia. And I think that when there's a humanitarian issue on the baseline, the answer is … yes … yes … and yes. Somebody's got to go in and do it, and it really falls at the feet of the US because of the country's weight, prestige and power. (Singer 2002: 175)

With Scott's vision driving the narrative, anxieties about the short- and long-term consequences of the military intervention are displaced, particularly as the soldiers on screen bear no resemblance to their disaffected, anxious and alienated cinematic antecedents in

Apocalypse Now and *Platoon.* Indeed, Scott is not interested in "back stories" for either the conflict or the characters – all information that is not directly related to the battle is eliminated (ibid.: 157). Thus, the soldiers in *Black Hawk Down* are professional, well trained and simply obeying orders. This "preferred" view of US soldiers is at once modern (in so far as it emphasizes their professionalism and technical know-how), and traditional (in so far as it underlines their "spirit" and courage under fire, and establishes their moral superiority through a now-familiar Orientalist strategy). Set against the well-meaning and disciplined US forces are hoards of ill-disciplined, gun-toting Somalis cast in none-too-subtle terms as marauding savages. This oppositional logic is especially clear in the scene where one of the Black Hawk helicopters crashes in Mogadishu, and the surviving pilot is left to fight off hundreds of surrounding Somalis. More important was the film's depiction of the infamous image of Sgt Durant's naked body being dragged through the streets of Mogadishu. In 1993, these images quashed American popular support for the mission, but in the hands of Scott in 2001, these images were resuscitated in order to reinforce the brutality, viciousness and immorality of the Somalis as compared to the honorable, selfless nobility of the Americans.

The retelling of "Operation Restore Hope" as a success was delivered to the audience in the classic style of war films – through claims of authenticity, realism and verisimilitude. Key to this effort was special effects supervisor Neil Corbould (who won an Academy Award for his "realistic" battle scenes in *Saving Private Ryan*) and the three military advisers who were on set to "keep it real" (Singer 2002: 170–1). While Col. Thomas Matthews claimed that *Black Hawk Down* was "frank and brutal and about as realistic as you can get," former Navy SEAL Harry Humphries went even further: "[Bruckheimer] is always looking for accuracy – as much as film will allow – and he's not going to compromise. He will always vote in favor of accuracy with respect to military or law enforcement activities, as opposed to the Hollywood view of how it should look" (Singer 2002: 159; Snead 2002). What Humphries assumes here – and what must be strongly resisted – is that accuracy is "disinterested rather than ideologically motivated" (Custen 1992: 11). In the case of *Black Hawk Down,* claims of accuracy and verisimilitude are carefully sustained by a prowar ideology. Commenting on its involvement in the film, the Army Public Affairs Office (APAO) explained: "We care if the project is historical, if it's accurate in its depiction of the Army… Obviously there are some scripts that, just by looking at, we know we can't support, like ones where the Army is in the employ of the Devil" (Snead 2002). In other words, such a position problematically asserts that war films that are critical of army personnel, procedures and actions – films like *M*A*S*H* that mobilize antiwar ideologies – *cannot* be historically accurate. According to the APAO, only approved (and therefore uncritical) depictions of the army – like that offered in *Black Hawk Down* – can be considered accurate.

Rather than politicize the ideological agenda behind *any* cinematic claim to accuracy, critics of *Black Hawk Down* focused on how its "biased" approach failed to provide a political context for the Somali crisis, failed to reveal the role of American oil companies in supporting dictator Said Barre's vicious regime in the 1980s, failed to depict the more "unfavorable" activities of the American soldiers (e.g. helicopter "rotor-washing" over Mogadishu, which tore the clothes off Somalis), and failed to explain that much of the famine was over by the time the UN and US troops arrived (Cox 2002; Monbiot 2002; Talbot 2002). In addition, critics focused on the Orientalist logic of *Black Hawk Down,* suggesting that the film was unapologetically racist because it glorified the American soldiers and dehumanized the Somalis. In his review for the *New York Times*, for example, Elvis Mitchell commented: "In *Black Hawk Down,* the lack of characterization converts the Somalis into a pack of snarling dark-skinned beasts, gleefully pulling the Americans from their downed aircraft and stripping them. Intended or not, it reeks of glumly staged racism" (2001). For George Monbiot, the racist logic of the film was further reinforced by the music: "[the Somalis] are accompanied by sinister Arab techno, while the US forces are trailed by violins, oboes and vocals inspired by Enya" (2002).

Given how these images of heroic Americans fighting menacing others reinforced already circulating stereotypes – particularly relevant in the nakedly patriotic mood following September 11th – it is hardly surprising that reaction to the film, in the US at least, was largely positive. Taking $108.6 million at the domestic box office, *Black Hawk Down* also drew fulsome praise from key members of the Bush administration: Dick Cheney, Donald Rumsfeld and Paul Wolfowitz all attended a gala Washington premiere of the film (Burlas 2002). While Wolfowitz's reaction was positive but vague ("It's a powerful film. I think it's good for this time. It reminds people what it's all about"), Sony Chairman Howard Stringer (the distributor of the film) was very clear that the film would "benefit from the US activity in Afghanistan" (Roberts 2002: C01). This is not to suggest that *Black Hawk Down* would have floundered without the events of September 11th; rather, that the largely promilitary, patriotic stance forged through an alliance between Scott, Bruckheimer and the Pentagon found even greater favor with a US public traumatized by what had happened in New York and Washington. If it was unsurprising that *Black Hawk Down* became a "cause celebre" for the traditional right in the politically reactionary mood of post-September 11th, it is perhaps also unsurprising that figures on what remained of the Left saw the film in very different terms. Many critics objected to its celebratory, gung-ho militarism, its offensive, explicit racism and its unproblematic view of a global political order in which America's preeminent position and moral virtuosity remained entirely unquestioned. These oppositional readings found public expression in the protests organized by a range of political activists and staged outside theaters where *Black Hawk Down* was being screened (Winkler 2002). For example, groups like ANSWER (Act Now to Stop War and End Racism) called on the public to boycott *Black Hawk Down*, and used negative reaction to the film as a way to "organize to build the anti-war movement" (ANSWER 2002).

While oppositional readings of the film jostled for exposure during a post-September 11th climate in America, the international reception of the film told a different story. Despite the increasing trend of Hollywood making more profits from overseas markets than domestic ones, *Black Hawk Down* was a relative failure at the international box office. It grossed $108.6 million in the domestic market (68.3%) but only $50.5 million in the international market (31.7%). Indeed, industry insiders made predictions that the film would take $141 million at the international box office – almost *three times* what it actually earned (Box Office Mojo 2002; Box Office Guru, 2003). More significantly perhaps, the success of the film in select markets overseas foreshadowed the geopolitical divisions that emerged in the post-September 11th global order. While *Black Hawk Down* was a massive success in the US and Australia (and a moderate success in the UK), in Japan, France and Germany it only achieved a very limited first-run release.[1] Still, the most revealing audience reaction came from the Somalis themselves who watched a premiere of sorts a mile from the Mogadishu battleground depicted in the film. As CNN reported, the reaction from the Somali crowd was diametrically opposed to the American response: "Audience members seemed to take delight in the scenes of U.S. defeat. Each time an American chopper went down in the film, the audience cheered. Every time an American serviceman was killed, the audience cheered some more" (Koinange 2002).

EMPIRE, POST-POLITICS AND META-SOVEREIGNTY

It is clear that the polemic debates about *Black Hawk Down* rehearsed in the previous section were able to mobilize audiences around established "right–left" political agendas. However, neither reading of the film engages with its articulation, reproduction and participation in a newly emerging global order. In other words, "Americentric" arguments about *Black Hawk Down* fail to show how the film dis-seminates networked, contingent and competing discourses that necessarily exceed, without wholly usurping, the autonomy and sanctity of "America" as a nation state. Drawing on critical scholars in political theory, international relations and cultural studies, we want to recast the "either/or" terms that have characterized popular debates about sovereignty and globalization, because it is precisely these terms that encourage polarized readings of *Black Hawk Down* and silence the difficult and complex discourses that emerge in the film's production, text and reception. *Black Hawk Down* is indicative of how Hollywood films participate in a newly emerging cultural, political, social, military and economic order whose authority is simultaneously dependent on state institutions and agencies and at the same time realized through a myriad of more diffuse and transnational networks of power. This is a significant film because it marks a new departure in Hollywood's engagement with questions of global politics: it expresses the concerns and ambitions not only of the world's only hegemon, but also of the decentered and fragmented order of rule described by Michael Hardt and Antonio Negri in *Empire*.

Hardt and Negri's analysis in *Empire* is instructive because it does not interpret global politics as a system in which tributes flow from peripheries to great capital cities (like the Roman or even the British Empire). "Our postmodern empire," we are told, "has no Rome" (2000: 317). Rather, Hardt and Negri envision global politics as "a decentered and deterritorializing apparatus of rule that progressively incorporates the entire global realm within its open, expanding frontiers" (ibid.: xii). For Hardt and Negri, this framework, in part, allows for a limited articulation of sovereign power: America does occupy a privileged position in Empire, but more significantly it challenges the idea that the global order "is dictated by a single power and a single center of rationality transcendent to global forces" (ibid.: 7). So when Hardt and Negri argue that "the U.S. world police acts not in imperialist interest but in imperial interest" their distinction is not just semantic (ibid.: 180). America no longer acts as a nineteenth-century colonial power, acquiring and settling territories, and establishing absolute differences between Self and Other, white and black, inside and outside, ruler and ruled. America's post-Vietnam interventions in global "trouble spots" like Somalia are justified not as a "seizures" of land in the service of colonial outposts, but as benign "police actions" in the interests of everyone that aim to eradicate conflict and difference, reconstruct social equilibrium, and incorporate the entire global realm within "a network of powers and counterpowers structured in a boundless and inclusive architecture"(ibid.: 166).

Hardt and Negri's analysis is instructive, then, because it articulates how and why our contemporary cultural, political, social, military and economic moment – what they call "Empire" – constitutes a break from nineteenth-century colonialism rather than an extension of it. However, like other critical readers of Hardt and Negri, we have reservations about letting go of the term "sovereignty" and wholeheartedly embracing their notion of "Empire" (Barkawi and Laffey 2003; Walker 2003; Laffey and Weldes 2004; Passavant and Dean 2004). Though Hardt and Negri speak about the newly emerging patterns of global order and the changed, deterritorialized, decentered nature of contemporary power formations, their concept of "Empire" departs too quickly from the nation state, particularly when the nation state in question is one as politically, culturally and militarily dominant as the US. As Laffey and Weldes argue, "The United States appears to hold 'the reins' of global military power, finance and communications, but Hardt and Negri claim – against the evidence – that this is not the case" (2004: 131). Laffey and Weldes go on to explain that sovereign borders are not quite as porous as Hardt and Negri seem to imagine, and that America's strategic use of international organizations like the UN has itself been well and truly jettisoned in the current "War on Terror" – all of which renders Hardt and Negri's claims about US multilateralism "wildly anachronistic" (ibid.). Along with other critical readers of *Empire,* we draw back from some of the more optimistic and utopian elements of Hardt and Negri's analysis whereby the "multitude" – "the productive, creative subjectivities of globalization" – have the capacity to transform Empire's modes of power and control for their own ends (2000: 166; Featherstone 2002). Some of the more repressive mechanisms utilized by the US within and beyond its own sovereign boundaries mean that the assimilation of the nation state – or at least one as powerful as the US – within this kind of globalized order will only ever be partial.

Hardt and Negri's analysis is most useful, then, not as some kind of political manifesto or catalyst for radical global political upheaval, but rather as a provocative account that astutely describes the numerous and increasingly diffuse ways in which power circulates simultaneously within national *and* global realms. Control, authority and legitimacy – both sovereign and otherwise – are achieved not through overt strategies of domination, but through an apparently disinterested, politically "neutral" emphasis on inclusion, the eradication of boundaries, management, expertise, professionalism and putting everyone and everything into its proper place. This is what Slavoj Zizek calls "post-politics": "the need to leave old ideological divisions behind and confront new issues, armed with the necessary expert knowledge and free deliberation that takes people's concrete needs and demands into account" (1999: 198). The term meta-sovereignty, then, speaks to, and about, two interlocking phenomena. First, drawing upon Zizek's notion of "post-politics" and Hardt and Negri's *Empire*, it articulates a general sense of the way in which new decentered formations of power are currently circulating in the global realm. Second, drawing from Laffey and Weldes, it calls attention to the dangers of downplaying "the continuing centrality of the state – and of one state in particular – to the contemporary international" (2004: 138). Meta-sovereignty holds onto Zizek's, and Hardt and Negri's analyses of the diffuse ways in which power operates in the global realm without handcuffing itself to an understanding of global politics that ignores the effects of (US) state-bound policies and directives. Whereas Zizek's analysis ends by suggesting that the nation state is itself colonized by the global corporation – "the colonizing power is no longer a nation-state but the global company itself" (1999: 216) – we cannot overlook the extent to which the nation state, though transformed by capitalist globalization, remains crucial in forging alliances and hierarchies that perpetuate social, political and economic inequalities.

In developing an account of meta-sovereignty through the intellectual debates instigated by *Empire,* the next section addresses

Black Hawk Down in ways that go beyond efforts to "read" Hollywood films as expressions of American hegemonic ambitions. To be sure, it identifies how power, in terms of the film's production, text and reception, works through a set of more diffuse global authorities than just sovereignty. At the same time, however, it stops short of arguing that power is so diffuse, so decentered, that it becomes impossible to talk in meaningful ways about how film is a vehicle for competing ideologies – some of which reinforce the power of the nation state. As we will see, it is not that ideology is somehow absent from *Black Hawk Down*; rather, it is that we need a new critical idiom to "see" how ideology is working in and through the film.

TECHNOLOGY, SPECTACLE AND THE FICTION OF NEUTRALITY

If the forces of production shape and inform the mode of representation, then these changes should manifest themselves in the form and content of particular films. Such a claim carries particular weight when considering the emergence of a distinctive type of Hollywood "blockbuster" film whose form, even more than its content, is dependent upon new technologies of production (e.g. computer-generated images) and whose very existence, given the enormous production and distribution costs involved, necessarily depends on new strategies of global financing and distribution. This is certainly the case with *Black Hawk Down,* whose financing, production and distribution inevitably exceeded the confines of the nation state. With this in mind, we are compelled to ask whether a film like *Black Hawk Down* actually ends up expressing the concerns and preoccupations of global authorities *other* than an imagined America. For example, for Sony and its multinational financiers, the importance of Scott's film is not primarily its ability to secure American hegemony, but rather its ability to promote a far more widespread, horizontally integrated entertainment portfolio including computer games, merchandizing and book and DVD tie-ins.

Thus, the production of Scott's film needs to be understood in the context of broader political, economic and cultural transformations currently affecting both national and global constituencies. Miller et al. make the point that Hollywood is at the forefront of contemporary shifts in global trade. As such, the industry is dependent on multinational financing, and benefits from free-trade agreements negotiated by the US government and the WTO.[2] The makers of *Black Hawk Down* took advantage of reduced trade barriers recently secured by the WTO and elected to film entirely on location in Morocco. While the shoot was beneficial to the Moroccan economy – an "official" source in the Moroccan government indicated that the film business had "poured" $200 million into the country in 2000 alone – the "real" winners of such arrangements are the film production companies (James 2002). Specifically, *Black Hawk Down's* makers received the following while in Morocco: an exemption from the 20 percent Euro

VAT tax on goods and services, full use of the Royal Moroccan Military and National police, same-day custom clearance for equipment, and access to 1,500 below-the-line, nonunionized film technicians willing to work longer hours for less wages than their Western counterparts (Vaucher 2002).

It is, of course, possible to argue that the relations currently developing between multinational film production companies, global authorities like the WTO and nation states unfairly advantage those countries and corporations with the necessary economic and political muscle to exploit these new arrangements. In the context of *Black Hawk Down*, then, it would be possible to argue that any benefits enjoyed by the Moroccan economy pale in comparison to the benefits enjoyed by particular global corporations and, given the importance of such corporations to the economic health of the United States, by the nation state of America as well.[3] However, to argue that Hollywood's financial domination of global cinema is only ever symbolic of American hegemony or the corresponding power of American-based corporations overlooks the extent to which hugely complex multinational financing and licensing arrangements are themselves transforming the nature of the Hollywood film industry. *Black Hawk Down*, made by the Los Angeles-based Revolution Studios, is symptomatic of the global nature of contemporary film production and distribution. Revolution's financing came from a series of arrangements made with Sony (its surrogate parent and distributor in the US and worldwide), Fox, Encore (who provided $150 million in equity funding), Pony Canyon and two "overseas" output partners – Germany's Senator Films and Japan's Toho-Towa (responsible for providing start-up finance and distribution in their "home" countries; Bloom 2002; Bart 2003). As such, the notion that American money finances American films is hopelessly outdated and, to use Rosenbaum's terms, it seems much more appropriate to talk about a "multinational" rather than a nationally "pure" cinema (2000: 133).

How, then, does the "multinational" context of production translate at the formal level of filmmaking? Blockbuster movies like *Black Hawk Down* have helped to make spectacle the new lingua franca of global cinema by manipulating cinematic esthetics in order to "shock and awe" audiences. Though spectacular images and action sequences do not transcend cultural and linguistic borders (i.e. film audiences in different parts of the world do not necessarily respond to such images in the same way), they are at least *accessible* to everyone. As such, blockbuster films have become a crucial medium of global communication – they are able to facilitate the production of consensus around contentious issues, debates and events in global politics. Such a claim is, of course, founded upon the assumption of popular film's preeminent status as a carrier of ideology. But even if we employ Ryan and Kellner's complex and critical understanding of ideology and popular film, it is by no means clear what happens when the formal conventions traditionally associated with Hollywood films

– "narrative closure, image continuity, nonreflexive camera, character identification, voyeuristic objectification, sequential editing, causal logic, dramatic motivation, shot centering, frame balance, realist intelligibility, etc." – are rearranged into spectacular action sequences with global appeal (Ryan and Kellner 1988: 1). How, in such cases, does ideology work? We are not suggesting that there has been a significant moment of rupture whereby "old" and "new" Hollywood constitute irrevocably opposed categories. However, if a new type of blockbuster film relies on different technologies of production (i.e. multinational) and comes to assume new formal characteristics as a result (i.e. the privileging of spectacle), then such films require a new critical idiom in order to determine how ideology is working. As Stam and Miller put it, "the old critiques of dominant cinema in terms of linear narrative, eyeline matches and invisible editing no longer quite 'work' since recent blockbuster cinema ... is less interested in verisimilitude and spatio-temporal integrity than in pure sensation" (2000: 228).

The key difference between Ryan and Kellner's analysis of traditional Hollywood films and Stam and Miller's description of recent blockbuster cinema is the extent to which the latter provides an account of spectacle. Here, Claudia Springer's argument that spectacular combat sequences in war films are "exemplary instances of cinematic excess" is particularly instructive (1988: 480). With their inevitable semiotic overload, these sequences are located outside the traditional "beginning-middle-end" story line and encourage audiences to experience "the pleasure of looking when it is unconstrained by narrative logic" (ibid.). Springer's point is that combat sequences in most war films are contained by a recuperative narrative framework which "explains" the film's ideological ambitions. Short, intense battle sequences realized by a range of formal devices (e.g. deafening sound effects, staccato dialogue, hand-held camera work, juxtaposed high/low shots and rapid editing) are followed by longer sequences that mark a return to conventional forms of narrative filmmaking (ibid.). For example, in the aftermath of a battle sequence, the audience's identification with particular individuals is reestablished by devices such as shot/reverse-shot editing, explicatory dialogue and narrative signposting. It is in these sequences, Springer argues, that a film's ideological position is developed and rendered accessible. As she concludes, "the onus for conveying [say] an antiwar message ultimately falls on the narrative, for it has to compensate for the more ambiguous signifying system of spectacle" (ibid.: 484).

With Springer's argument in mind, *Black Hawk Down* might seem like quite a conventional war film. Employing a familiar range of formal devices (e.g. grainy film stock, dull desert colors, hand-held camera work, reliance on a range of "character actors" rather than one recognizable star, and the conjunction of rapid-fire editing, long shots and low-angle/high-angle "helicopter" shots) these sequences operate according to the logic of spectacular excess as outlined by

Springer. It is hard, when watching the film, not to succumb to the intensity of the combat experience. "That's my job," Scott claims, "it's what I do ... putting the audience actually in the scene in the delivery and on the receiving end. Making them feel it" (Foden 2002). In order to make audiences "feel" rather than think about what they are watching, Scott produces "two-and-a-quarter hours of directionless, cacophonous kick-ass operatics," rather than a carefully paced narrative with established characters, causal logic or "realist" intelligibility (Bradshaw 2002). Telling, in this respect, is Scott's reaction to the audience at the opening night screening in Leicester Square in London: "he was watching the backs of heads and was pleased to see that nobody moved" (Barber 2002). What differentiates Scott's film from others in the war-film genre is the *extent* to which spectacle is in excess of the narrative. Whereas spectacular combat sequences in most war films are contained by a coherent narrative that gives the film order and meaning, the fifty-minute middle section of *Black Hawk Down*, which details the incursion into Mogadishu, is accompanied by little or no narrative explanation. These scenes contain almost no dialog and are little more than spectacular cinematic amalgamations of gunfire, running soldiers, evocative music, swarming Somalis and crashing helicopters. Underlining this sense of difference, the film's production notes explain that "[u]nlike many action films, in which scenes are shot in 30- to 45-second segments, Scott preferred filming long, complex combat sequences from beginning to end, with cameras capturing specific moments as per their placement" (Singer 2002: 169).

Our point is that because these sequences are not framed and hence explained by an anchoring narrative that orders and directs audience responses, it is all but impossible to locate any clear ideological commitment in them. The very fact that the film simultaneously manages to be antiwar (i.e. "look at the destruction and loss of life ... isn't war terrible?") and prowar (i.e. "war is necessary and aren't the US soldiers doing a good, professional job?") is less a testament to the constantly shifting nature of ideology than it is to the ability of spectacle to reconcile and displace contrasting political viewpoints. To paraphrase Scott, powerful spectacles of action and violence make us "feel" the experience of combat rather than "think" about its political ramifications. In this sense, the film's willingness to foreground spectacle at the expense of narrative installs what Mark Lacy refers to as a "view from everywhere," or conversely a view from nowhere in particular, which serves to alleviate moral responsibility (2003: 620). As such, our claim is not simply that spectacle in *Black Hawk Down* constitutes "an ambiguous signifying system" whereby audiences necessarily respond in different ways due to a lack of narrative signposting. Rather, as we demonstrate below, spectacular action sequences in the film have been recuperated into new hegemonic systems and matrices of deterritorialized power.

For Mark Bowden, author of the original *Black Hawk Down* that became the source material for Scott's film, this apparent neutrality or absence of politics is one of the film's strengths:

> Some journalists and critics have labored mightily to find the political message of the film, but there isn't one. At heart, it is the story of a group of young soldiers who desperately want to experience battle and who get their wish. The best stories are not those that lecture us about politics or history, but which connect with us on a visual level. (Bowden 2002: xii)

In one sense, Bowden and Scott are right to argue that *Black Hawk Down* is not a political film, at least in the usual understanding of this term. The film, for example, provides no coherent pro- or antiwar message, nor does it appear to explicitly validate or critique traditional forms of American power. However, Scott's self-confessed desire to render the "reality" of the combat experience largely through technical decisions about how to shoot particular scenes – and consequently the film's near-total reliance on spectacular action sequences to best convey a sense of "what it was really like" in Somalia – is not a neutral position. This simultaneous view from everywhere and nowhere is deeply political, but in a way that needs to be contextualized within the meta-sovereign framework that we have set out in this article. *Black Hawk Down* has no center, and no conventional narrative anchors; rather, it articulates and is articulated by diffuse, decentered and deterritorialized circulations of power that secure particular interests (i.e. of America) even as an apparently neutral or disinterested position is being constructed (i.e. a "just" intervention for the good of all). The "real" hegemonic force here is the collusion between spectacular action sequences unbounded by narrative logic and providing no coherent political content, and a particular kind of neoliberal politics in which everyone's opinions are listened to and assimilated into a complex hierarchical chain of command. Just as the film's privileging of spectacle over narrative enables Scott, falsely, to absolve himself of political responsibility, its problematic claim of telling an "objective" and "accurate" story overlooks the extent to which the global arrangement of sovereign power means that certain national stories (i.e. those of the US soldiers) are necessarily more important than others (i.e. those of the Somalis).

Scott's excessive privileging of spectacle and claims of neutrality constitute a new departure in Hollywood's engagement with the "realities" of war. However, such a strategy manifests itself not simply through cinematic form but also in terms of content – how Scott sets up and appears to resolve thematic conflicts within the film itself. The generic conventions of Hollywood war films are structured around a series of tensions and oppositions whereby the desires and concerns of a particular figure are at odds with those of the group that he is a part of, or the cause he is representing. War films resolve these tensions and oppositions so that, in the end, audiences do not have to choose between competing value systems or mythologies (e.g. between the imperatives of individualism on the one hand, and submitting oneself to a collective cause on the other). Where a war film refuses to make clear-cut choices between different categories or values (e.g. *The Thin Red Line*), the resultant confusion and ambivalence are politically engaging in so far as they resist the type of will to order that, in Zizek's terms, seeks perpetual harmony and brings about what he calls the end of "politics proper."

One of the structuring thematic tensions in *Black Hawk Down* is illuminated in the following exchange between Eversmann and Mike Kurth (Gabriel Casseus) over their respective attitudes toward the Somalis – or the "skinnies" – during preparations for the incursion into Mogadishu:

Eversmann: It's not that I like them or don't like them. I respect them.

Kurth: See, what you guys fail to realize is, Sergeant here is a bit of an idealist. He believes in the mission down to his very bones. Don't you, Sergeant?

Eversmann: Look, these people have no jobs, no formal education, no future. I just figure that, you know what I mean, we have two things we can do. We can either help or we can sit back and watch the country destroy itself on CNN. Right?

Kurth: I don't know about you guys but I was trained to fight. Were you trained to fight, Sarge?

Eversmann: Well, I think I was trained to make a difference.

This exchange, aired to other soldiers who effectively function as arbiters, brings this central thematic tension into relief. On one side, then, is Kurth, the trained soldier "just doing his job" – not thinking but doing – and on the other side is Eversmann, the idealist, who speaks about the ethics of intervention. Rather than being irreconcilable positions that the film must work hard to resolve, these tensions are falsely constructed. Both positions are effectively the same, or rather part of the same concern – that of fighting a "just" war. For Hardt and Negri, the concept of a "just" war has traditionally comprised two distinctive, diverging strands: "the banalization of war" (this is effectively Kurth's position) and the "celebration of war as an ethical instrument" (Evermann's position; 2000: 12). *Black Hawk Down* represents a new political and cultural moment when both these tenets are synthesized into one. As Hardt and Negri suggest: "These two traditional characteristics have reappeared in our postmodern world: on the one hand, war is reduced to the status of police action, and on the other, the new power that can legitimately exercise ethical function through war is sacrilized" (ibid.).

With Hardt and Negri's comments in mind, the task of reconciling the views put forward by Kurth and Eversmann is straightforward because both are part of the same preoccupation: war as a routine police action (with America as global policeman) and war as a sacralized function of a new ethical authority (with America acting in the interest of a "universal" good). As if to underline this synthesis, their exchange is respectful and humorous and the listening soldiers nod in tacit agreement when both men speak. Significantly, too, the question of consequences (e.g. the consequences of this "ethical" intervention for the Somalis in terms of, say, loss of life) is studiously avoided and the film strives to wrap things up by simultaneously emphasizing the *rightness* of the action and the importance, from the soldier's point of view, of "not thinking." As "Hoot" Gibson (Eric Bana) says to Eversmann after their arrival at the UN-protected stadium has been joyfully received by grateful Somali children: "It's about me next to you. That's it. That's all it is." Reminiscent of Scott's own ambitions as a filmmaker, soldiers are to act in a detached, professional manner, and fulfil the Ranger's code (and tagline of the film): "leave no man behind."

In many ways, *Black Hawk Down* articulates Hardt and Negri's boundless, centerless model of global political authority and Zizek's idea of post-politics whereby "the conflict of global ideological visions embodied in different parties which compete for power" is collapsed and replaced by a cabal of enlightened technocrats and politicians who reach a compromise "in the guise of a more or less universal consensus" (Zizek 1999: 198). However, this approach is not quite able to speak to, and about, a situation in which the strategies of control practiced by the US troops are not invisible (as Hardt and Negri would have us believe) but rather aggressively coercive and, in part, modeled on the repressive policing practices undertaken by various US agencies within and beyond American borders. Our point is that such practices replicate neither the bald logic of an uncomplicated American imperialism (whereby the Somalis are to be identified and conquered) nor the diffuse, decentered logic of Hardt and Negri's "Empire" (where the Somalis are to be tolerated and managed). Rather, *Black Hawk Down* reimagines America as the head of "a complex and unevenly developed internationalized state apparatus for policing…modeled on and influenced by the United States and with local, national, regional, international, and transnational manifestations" (Laffey and Weldes 2004: 137). This is akin to our understanding of meta-sovereignty in so far as it allows for the articulation of political control that draws upon both a neoliberal preoccupation with inclusion, flexibility and management as well as the coercive practices employed by various US military agencies. As such, the film's depiction of the Somalis as both mute victims (and hence needing US protection) and marauding savages (and hence a threat to the ethical order) is best understood *not* as an example of unreconstructed racism, but rather as an expression of the uneasy tension between liberal and repressive imperatives at work in contemporary global politics. Just as the film subsumes US forces into a larger UN cohort, so too does the US claim to act "for freedom loving people everywhere" – including places like Somalia. But this idea of a benevolent, multinational "coalition of the willing" is deconstructed in the film as professional, dedicated and heroic US troops are counterposed against their allies. For example, the film makes it clear that part of the delay in evacuating the Black Hawk survivors was due to the unhelpful and reluctant Pakistani peacekeepers who were slow to respond to America's request for help. In effect, national interest is never entirely absent from even the most multinational force pursuing the most humanitarian goals.

CONCLUSION

In the shift from a sovereign to a meta-sovereign framework, the distinctions of previously dialectical categories – inside/outside, universal/particular, America/world – have collapsed in the face of power formations and flows that are not fixed and state-bound, but mobile, flexible and networked. In such a brave new world, Hollywood films are both an indicator of and a vehicle for transformation. That is to say, they simultaneously emphasize and secure America's right to intervene as it sees fit, and speak about the ways in which sovereign boundaries have been unsettled by new global power formations. On the one hand, then, *Black Hawk Down* was used to address public concerns about the rightness of invading Afghanistan in early 2002; on the other hand the film recasts the relationship between America ("the particular") and the world ("the universal") so as to unsettle sovereign conceptions of the way in which power functions.[4] That is, it addresses Zizek's question of what happens when "the Universal emerges within the Particular when some particular content starts to function as the stand-in for the absent Universal" (1999: 176). In terms of what we have been arguing in this article, then, America's claims to universality – America functioning "as the stand-in for the absent universal" – do not lead inevitably to the creation of a world formed in its image. Rather, just as the world is recast in America's image, American sovereignty is transformed by its immersion in global affairs. This is not to say that American military, political and economic power is somehow illusory; rather, the way in which that power is exercised in a globalized world, and America's relationship with that globalized world, has fundamentally transformed.

By way of conclusion, we want to think about the implications of these changes for the way in which blockbuster Hollywood films are produced, made and watched more generally. Certainly it is clear that the changing nature of film financing, production and distribution has inevitably affected what gets made and how it gets made, and that the effects of such changes will continue to make themselves felt in the future. Additionally, the privileging of spectacle over coherent political commitment and the resultant implications for the ways in which films are viewed will, unfortunately from our perspective, continue apace. The particular case of *Black Hawk Down*, in fact, offers quite an unpalatable metaphor for the future of Hollywood cinema. As such, the mantra of the soldiers – it's all about doing rather than thinking – becomes Scott's leitmotif as filmmaker: he wants to get the technical "stuff" right and leave the politics for someone else to think about. The end result, as with the Somalia intervention itself, constitutes something of a mess – for who, or what, is calling the shots in this film? The producer? The director? The global financiers? The imagined needs of a global audience? And how are these concerns themselves implicated in, and shaped by, the kinds of changes to the global political, economic and cultural order that we have addressed in this paper? Is it enough to say that *Black Hawk Down* is "great to look at," and leave it at that? Our concern is that once power is characterized as diffuse and fragmented, what emerges is *not* the rule of a single center of rationality, but the rule of no one, or no one and everyone at the same time. And this, of course, poses extremely difficult questions about responsibility. The ambivalence of *Black Hawk Down,* and the fact that it articulates so many contrary positions, is indicative of our current political climate. The reasons for global intervention – as we saw with Iraq in 2003 – are as slippery and contingent as the networks of power sustaining the current global order, even as these networks are able to secure and augment American hegemonic ambitions.

NOTES

The authors would like to thank John Armitage and four anonymous reviewers for their helpful comments and suggestions.

1. *Variety* reported that *Black Hawk Down* opened in Germany "with a less than stellar box office take of $971,525 in the first weekend" (Meza 2002); the magazine also reported that the film "failed to grip in Japan" (Schwarzacher 2003). As a result of these poor performances, Revolution's output partners in Germany and Japan renegotiated the terms of their contracts "down."
2. Miller et al. argue that "Today, perhaps the greatest force working for … Hollywood's geographical command over the [New International Cultural Division of Labour] is the World Trade Organization" (2001: 34).
3. Henry A. Giroux estimates that the entertainment industry "is [America's] second largest export industry – second only to military aircraft" (2002: 11).
4. Significantly, once the attacks had taken place, Sony made a deal with the US military to ship copies of the film to bases in Afghanistan in order to bolster troop morale (Dorio 2002).

REFERENCES

ANSWER: 2002. "Protest *Black Hawk Down*." Available online: www.internationalanswer.org/news/update/011802blackhawkdown.html.

Ashley, R. and Walker, R.B.J. (eds). 1990. *International Studies Quarterly* [special edition]. 34(3).

Balakrishnan, G. (ed.). 2003. *Debating Empire.* London: Verso.

Barber, L. 2002. "Scott's Corner." *The Observer,* 6 January.

Barkawi, T. 2004. "Globalization, Culture, and War: On the Popular Mediation of 'Small Wars'." *Cultural Critique,* 58, special issue (forthcoming).

Barkawi, T. and Laffey, M. 2003. "Retrieving the Imperial: *Empire* and International Relations." *Millennium: Journal of International Studies,* 31(1): 109–27.

Bart, P. 2003. "Roth's Revolutionary rites." *Variety,* 5 May.

Bloom, D. 2002. "Soph focus at revolution." *Variety,* 18 January.

Bowden, M. 2002. "Forward." In Ken Nolan (ed.), *Black Hawk Down: The Shooting Script.* New York: Newmarket Press, pp. vii–xv.

Box Office Guru. 2003. "Worldwide Box Office Grosses." Available online: www.boxofficeguru.com/intlarch1.htm.

Box Office Mojo. 2002. "International Weekend Report." 18 January. Available online: www.boxofficemojo.com/intl/weekend/011802. htm.

Bradshaw, P. 2002. "*Black Hawk Down* (Review)." *The Guardian,* 18 January.

Burchill, G., Gordon, C. and Miller, P. (eds). 1991. *The Foucault Effect: Studies in Governmentality.* Chicago: University of Chicago Press.

Burlas, J. 2002. "*Black Hawk Down* reflects Army values." *Public Affairs: US Army.* Available online: www.dtic.mil/armylinks/news/Jan2002/a20020116bhdown.html.

Camilleri, J. and Falk, J. 1992. *The End of Sovereignty.* Aldershot: Edward Elgar.

—— 1992. *Writing Security: United States" Foreign Policy and the Politics of Identity.* Manchester: Manchester University Press.

—— 1998. *National Deconstruction: Violence, Identity and Justice in Bosnia.* Minneapolis: University of Minnesota Press.

Carruthers, S.L. 2003. "Bringing it All Back Home: Hollywood Returns to War." *Small Wars and Insurgencies,* 14(1): 167–82.

Cockburn, A. 2002. "Wild Justice: Black Hawk Bilge." *New York Press,* 15(3). Available online: www.nypress.com/15/3/news&columns/wildjustice.cfm.

Cox, A. 2002. "Black Hawk Down: Shoot first, don't ask questions later." *The Independent,* 12 January.

Custen, G. 1992. *Bio/Pics: How Hollywood Constructed Public History.* New Brunswick: Rutgers University Press.

Der Derian, J. 1992. *Antidiplomacy: Speed, Spies and Terror in International Relations.* Oxford: Blackwell.

—— 2001. *Virtuous War: Mapping the Military-Industrial-Media-Entertainment Network.* Boulder: Westview Press.

Der Derian, J. and Shapiro, M. (eds). 1989. *International/Intertextual Relations: Postmodern Readings of World Politics.* Lexington: Lexington Books.

Dillon, M. 2004. "From Geopolitics to Biopolitics: Correlating sovereign and biopower." In J. Edkins, V. Pin-fat and M. Shapiro (eds), *Sovereign Lives: Grammars of Power in an Era of Globalization*, pp. 65–93. London: Routledge.

Dillon, M. and Reid, J. 2000. "Global Governance, Liberal Peace, and Complex Emergencies." *Alternatives,* 25(1): 117–43.

—— 2001. "Global Liberal Governance: Biopolitics, Security and War." *Millennium: Journal of International Studies,* 30(1): 41–66.

Dorio, C. 2002. "Hawks hover atop Bowl-bashed B.O." *Variety,* 4 February.

Edkins, J., Pin-Fat, V. and Shapiro, M. (eds). 2004. *Sovereign Lives: Grammars of Power in an Era of Globalization.* London: Routledge.

Featherstone, M. 2002. "Empire and Utopia: A Psychoanalytic Critique of Totality." *Journal for Cultural Research,* 6(4): 369–84.

Foden, G. 2002. "You can't diddle with the truth." *The Guardian,* 11 January.

Foucault, M. 1972. *The Archaeology of Knowledge.* New York: Pantheon Books.

Fryer, J. 2002. "Jingoism Jibe over *Black Hawk Down.*" *BBC News,* 21 January. Available online: www.bbc.co.uk/1/hi/world/africa/1773466.stm.

Gaydos, S. 2001. "Can Bruckheimer's Hawk find place among Euro Doves?" *Variety,* 10 December.

George, J. 1994. *Discourses of Global Politics: A Critical (Re)introduction to International Relations.* Boulder: Lynne Reinner.

Giroux, H. 2002. *Breaking In To Movies: Film and the Culture of Politics.* Oxford: Blackwell.

Hall, S. 1993. "Encoding, Decoding." In S. During (ed.), *The Cultural Studies Reader.* London: Routledge, pp. 90–103.

Hardt, M. and Negri, A. 2000. *Empire.* Cambridge: Harvard University Press.

Hindess, B. 1996. *Discourses of Power: From Hobbes to Foucault.* Oxford: Oxford University Press.

Hirst, P. and Thompson, G. 1996. *Globalization in Question: The International Economy and the Possibilities of Governance.* Cambridge: Polity.

Hjort, M. and McKenzie, S. (eds). 2000. *Cinema and Nation.* London: Routledge.

Hozic, A. 2001. *Hollyworld: Space, Power and Fantasy in the American Economy.* Ithaca: Cornell University Press.

James, A. 2002. "Morocco to tap into Hollywood epic plans." *Variety,* 15 September.

Koinange, J. 2002. "Somalis cheer at *Black Hawk Down* screening." *CNN,* 22 January. Available online: www.edition.cnn.com/2002/WORLD/africa/01/22/blackhawk.screening/index.html.

Kolker, R. 2000. 3rd edn. *A Cinema of Loneliness.* Oxford: Oxford University Press.

Lacy, M. 2003. "War, Cinema, and International Relations." *Alternatives,* 28(5): 611–36.

Laffey, M. and Weldes, J. 2004. "Representing the International: Sovereignty after Modernity?" In Paul A. Passavant and Jodi Dean (eds), *Empire's New Clothes: Reading Hardt and Negri,* pp. 121–42. London: Routledge.

Lisle, D. 2003. "Screening Global Conflict." *International Feminist Journal of Politics,* 5(1): 134–41.

—— 2005. "Globalization." In I. McKenzie (ed.), *Political Concepts: A Reader and a Guide.* Edinburgh: Edinburgh University Press.

McCrisken, T. and Pepper, A. 2005. *American History and Contemporary Hollywood Film.* Edinburgh: Edinburgh University Press.

Mann, M. 1997. "Has Globalization Ended the Rise and Rise of the Nation State?" *Review of International Political Economy,* 4(3): 472–96.

Meza, E. 2002. "Senator Pacts with Kirch for Pics." *Variety,* 8 October.

Miller, T., Govil, N., McMuria, J. and Maxwell, R. (eds). 2001. *Global Hollywood.* London: BFI.

Mitchell, E. 2001. "Mission of Mercy Goes Bad in Africa." *New York Times,* 28 December.

Monbiot, G. 2002. "Both Saviour and Victim: *Black Hawk Down* Creates a New and Dangerous Myth of American Nationhood." *The Guardian,* 29 January.

Ohmae, K. 1996. *The End of the Nation State.* New York: Harper Collins.

Passavant, P.A. and Dean, J. (eds). 2004. *Empire's New Clothes: Reading Hardt and Negri.* London: Routledge.

Roberts, R. 2002. "Washington Brass Help Trumpet Black Hawk Down." *Washington Post,* 16 January: C01.

Rosenbaum, J. 2000. *Movie Wars: How Hollywood and the Media Limit What Films We Can See.* London: Wallflower Press.

Ryan, M. and Kellner, D. 1988. *Camera Politica: The Politics and Ideology of Contemporary Hollywood Film.* Bloomington: Indiana University Press.

Schwarzacher, L. 2003. "H'wood eclipses local fare." *Variety,* 17 February.

Sexton III, B. 2002. "What's Wrong with *Black Hawk Down.*" *The Socialist Worker,* 22 February. Available online: www.socialistworker. org/2002–1/395/395_08_BrendanSexton.shtml.

Shapiro, M.J. 1999. *Cinematic Political Thought: Narratives of Race, Nation and Gender.* New York: New York University Press.

—— 2002. "Wanted, Dead or Alive." *Theory and Event,* 5(4). Available online: www.muse.jhu.edu/journals/tae/toc/archive.html#5.4.

Singer, M. 2002. "Production Notes, Leave No Man Behind: The Making of *Black Hawk Down.*" In K. Nolan (ed.), *Black Hawk Down: The Shooting Script,* pp. 151–75. New York: Newmarket Press.

Snead, E. 2002. "The Special Operation of *Black Hawk Down:* Hollywood and the Military Join Forces." *The Washington Post,* 11 January.

Springer, C. 1988. "Antiwar Film as Spectacle: Contradictions in the Combat Sequence." *Genre*, 21(4): 479–86.

Stam, R. and Miller, T. (eds). 2000. *Film and Theory: An Anthology*. Oxford: Blackwell.

Talbot, A. 2002. "*Black Hawk Down*: naked propaganda masquerading as entertainment." *World Socialist Website*, 19 February, www.wsws.org/articles/2002/feb2002/hawk-f19.shtml.

Vaucher, A.R. 2002. "Moroccan fest touts local production." *Variety*, 22 September.

Walker, R.B.J. 1993. *Inside/Outside: International Relations as Political Theory*. Cambridge: Cambridge University Press.

—— 2003. "On the Immanence/Imminence of Empire." *Millennium: Journal of International Studies*, 31(2): 337–45.

Walsh, D. 2001. "Hollywood enlists in Bush's war drive." *World Socialist Website*, 19 November, www.wsws.org/articles/2001/nov2001/holl-n19.shtml.

Walsh, D.C. 2002. "Life Imitates Art Imitates Life... And Death." *Military Training Technology Online*, www.mt2–kmi.com.Archives/7_2_MT2/7_2_Art2.cfm.

Winkler, P. 2002. "(Feminist) Activism Post September 11: Protesting *Black Hawk Down*." *International Feminist Journal of Politics*, 4(3): 415–30.

Zizek, S. 1999. *The Ticklish Subject: The Absent Centre of Political Ontology*. London: Verso.

CULTURAL POLITICS   VOLUME 1, ISSUE 2   REPRINTS AVAILABLE   PHOTOCOPYING   © BERG 2005
                     PP 193–214   DIRECTLY FROM THE   PERMITTED BY LICENSE   PRINTED IN THE UK
                                           PUBLISHERS.   ONLY

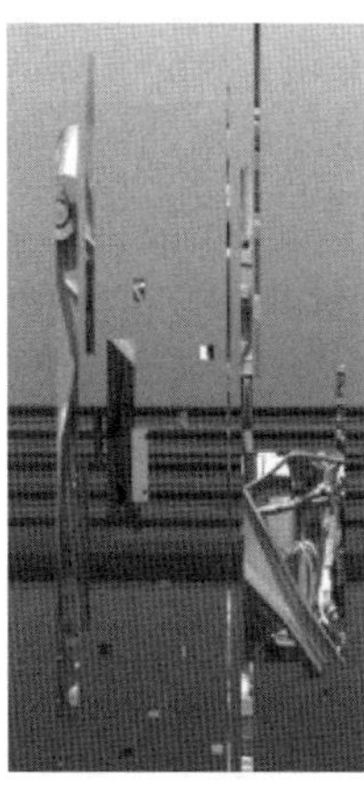

DISTRIBUTION AND MEDIA FLOWS

SEAN CUBITT

SEAN CUBITT IS PROFESSOR OF SCREEN AND MEDIA STUDIES AT THE UNIVERSITY OF WAIKATO, HAMILTON, AOTEAROA, NEW ZEALAND. HE IS THE AUTHOR AND EDITOR OF SEVERAL BOOKS INCLUDING *DIGITAL AESTHETICS* (SAGE 1998), *SIMULATION AND SOCIAL THEORY* (SAGE 2001), *THE CINEMA EFFECT* (MIT 2004) AND *ECOMEDIA* (RODOPI 2005).

ABSTRACT   While production, text and audience have been extensively covered by media and cultural studies scholars, the study of distribution is in its infancy. This essay argues that the distributive moment of the media cycle – incorporating delivery to audiences, business-to-business distribution and the redistribution of profits and information derived from audiences – is critical to an understanding of twenty-first-century cultural politics. It offers an analysis of distribution, and considerations on the politics of alternative modes of distribution.

WHY DISTRIBUTION?

Distribution is the core process in which economic and political moments of human communication take center stage. The management of product, payment and data flows between producers and audiences have however rarely been addressed in media studies terms other than regulation and control, with other aspects left to the instrumental disciplines of marketing and public relations. Even the media economics textbooks of Doyle (2002) and Albarran (2002) have no entry for distribution in their contents or indexes. The lack of address to distribution derives from perspectives on media and mediation emphasizing culture, power, economics, indeed anything but what is here taken as the central fact of human action: communication in general and its materialization as media in particular. In this perspective, all mediation engages in commerce in its broadest sense – in the gift, in trade and barter, wherever in history people have exchanged things, favors or ideas. Modern distribution is characterized by its commodity form; contemporary exchange by its readiness to rework time as a raw material for the construction of markets, to play stasis against change, and to organize space hierarchically. Distribution is that function which organizes information in space and time, accelerating or delaying its delivery in spaces that it differentiates on that basis. In this sense distribution is the construction of difference; initially in distinguishing producer from audience, buyer from seller, and in a networked world further distinguishing and dividing populations by their temporal and spatial proximity to the economic power and political economy that is increasingly centralized, not at the site of production, but on the terrains of exchange. Critical to an understanding of contemporary cultural politics, distribution remains largely unanalyzed. The purpose of such analysis is to provide the grounds for an alternative cultural politics grounded in alternative models of distribution.

Producers produce use-values; audiences provide attention-value,[1] creating both meanings and information about themselves, but crucially also working, unpaid, to produce the attention bought and sold by advertisers (Smythe 1994). Distribution is the site of production of exchange-value and thus of profit. Distribution is also the material ground of cultural dominance and political power. In the history of the dominant media of the last hundred years, distributors have been responsible for founding the economic empires of network radio (Douglas 1987), TV (Barnouw 1982; Smith 1995), film studios (Gomery 1986), telecommunications (Kieve 1973; Fischer 1992) and internet services (Schiller 1999). The hunger of film, broadcast and electronic distributors for content led them to acquire the means of production, production that, in the media industries, is largely determined by the success of previous products in distribution: what has not found a market in the past will not get distributed in the future. Likewise, governments throughout the twentieth century have been alert to the uses of censorship, not only as a means to power, but also as an exercise of power in itself. That power today lies more generally in the hands of media corporations. The powers of both transnational corporations and governments can be defined as their ability to direct and delay the flow of mediation. Communication is the ground bass of society. Struggles over control of its flow are struggles over control of the social. That struggle takes place on the material ground of mediation: the material processes of communication.

In the narrower sense of negotiation by means of a go-between, in the broader sense of the life cycle of the media industry and in the broadest sense of the materiality of communication, the process of mediation is integrated, and distinctions between producing, distributing and the work of audiencing are to some extent artifacts of analysis rather than ontological categories. Nonetheless, such analysis is vital, given the scale and complexity of the mediation process. Marx is adamant that distribution and exchange, absorbed into the single category of distribution in the media industries and in the terminology adopted here, are subsidiary moments of production (Marx 1973: 96–9). Historically, the media industries have moved away from the production-centered economies of the nineteenth century, in one way proving Marx's theses that "Production is always a *particular* branch of production" (ibid.: 91; emphasis in original), and that when "Distribution steps between the producers and the products" (ibid.: 94), the process is one of mutual mediation (ibid.: 91). The commodity form has a history, one in which the role of distribution has come to have an increasingly central role, for example in the form of companies based exclusively on branding (Klein 2000) and intellectual property (IP). In this process the alienation of creative labor in IP is indistinguishable from the alienation of physical labor power in exchange-value in Marx's nineteenth century. Although objectively distribution cannot be divorced from production and consumption, in daily life that abstraction occurs in every economic act involving IP, from trademarks to industrial designs. Distribution thus articulates producers and consumers, but does so by representing each to the other in "the fantastic form of a relation between things" (Marx 1976: 165).

Because distribution is the moment of flows between the other poles, it is uniquely vulnerable to regulation. Media production and audiencing are open to creativity, and to that extent, within the limits of institutional and ideological constraints, they are free. Indeed It is their freedom that makes them valuable, since the free creativity of producers and audiences is the labor from which the distributive moment extracts exchange-value, in the form of everything from appreciation indexes to bug reporting. Distribution is responsible not only for intervening between but also for managing the relationships of consumers and producers: the acceleration and delay, promotion and restriction, the spatiotemporal orchestration of flows. People communicate freely, but that communication is everywhere in chains. Audiences do not simply consume media artifacts: they attend to them, make sense of them, pay for them and, under contemporary conditions, consolidate into markets for them. The processes that bring media to audiences, and that return audience response and money back to production are both integral to and distinguishable within the wider process of mediation. Bought, borrowed, bartered, stolen or given, the object must somehow arrive. Production, centered on craft and technologies that embed older craft, and audiencing, grounded in recognizing and making meaning, only appear as political-economic activities when seen from the point of view of distribution. The projected purchase by a Sony-led consortium of MGM-United Artists' 4,100 film and 10,000 episode TV libraries includes as a member Comcast, a US cable company with 22 million subscribers. Comcast alone is not included in the buyout of other consortium members, because it will supply the critical video-on-demand delivery of the library to premium consumers, likewise managing the onward sale of titles to less privileged markets through terrestrial networks (*Economist* 2004: 68). Sony is already the owner of Columbia-TriStar studios, in a deliberate maneuver to ensure that it never again faces exclusion from the domestic equipment market for lack of content to distribute (Lardner 1987). This large-scale but nonetheless typical conglomeration indicates the centrality of distribution to both content and hardware. For this reason, distribution is associated with the economic axis in Figure 1.

A materialist philosophy of mediation deals with relations between the physical, dimensional and informational aspects of the world. Mutually dependent (as in the energy cost of structure, or the bending of space by mass), they are nonetheless distinctive, as is the case with the moments of mediation. Communication involves three tasks, each a source of value. The technological mediation of matter and energy in space and time produces objects. The work of audiencing (the neologism is intended to stress that it is work) deploys technique (styles, conventions, icons...) to mediate between matter-energy and the informational apex, here characterized as

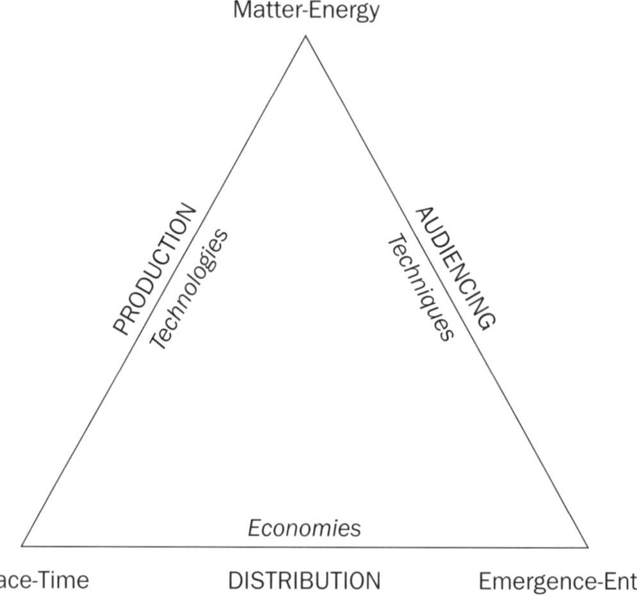

Figure 1

a relation between homeostasis and change, whether entropic or emergent. The distributive is the exchange of information across time and space. Some financial transactions, for example, move far more swiftly when a bank is being paid than when an individual is waiting for a check to clear. And the US–Mexico border can be traversed far more quickly going South than North. Such is the typical intervention of distribution in the organization of space and time, space as time.

The diagram (Figure 1) shows a moment when audience and producer meet directly in the physical object. At that moment, given the diminishing role of face-to-face communication in contemporary life, both producer and audience are most frequently imaginary constructs of one another. An author implies a reader in the text, and a reader infers an author. To some extent the economic exchange between dimensional and informational moments is equally fictive, in its de-emphasis of the exchange of physical product, and also because the work of distributing has characteristics of both production (the manufacture of exemplars) and audiencing (as when TV executives rely on "gut reaction" identifications with their audience in program purchasing). Today the famed instincts of industry heroes like Irving Thalberg (Fitzgerald's "Great Gatsby") are more likely to be supplied from the business-to-business sector through agencies like webstrendslive, specialists in tracking websurfers through cookie technology, or market research firms like AC Nielson. Likewise the nose of the old-time showmen for a possible market opening has been overwhelmed by global film and television markets like MIP-TV and MIP-COM, and ballyhoo by PR agencies. Increasingly alienated from the creative moments of production and audiencing, distribution has become the critical moment of their control in regimes of power and commodification. Though we might otherwise hope, with Habermas (1993), for universal well-being as a result of communication, emphasizing the regulation and commodification of both media products and audiences casts light on the origins of ignorance, poverty and oppression.

CONCEPTUALIZING DISTRIBUTION

Perhaps one reason why distribution has received relatively little attention is that in information theory it is the channel through which media are delivered. In Shannon and Weaver's mathematical theory, the channel is insignificant: only sending and receiving are vital. Distribution is in this sense a "black box." Media critique that has addressed the nature of channels has in general taken a McLuhanite line: the channel matters to the extent that it is determining of the message, and therefore of the positions of sender and receiver.[2] Slightly more sophisticated variants of sender-receiver theory, from the "uses and gratifications" school of mass communication to technologically literate theories of emergence, ascribe either transparency or agency to the technologies of communication, without addressing their economic and regulative functions. Textual models, like Schatz's (1981) famous triangular model of production, text and reader, again elide the moment of distribution, and in so doing reduce the complexity of the productive and the audience moments. His model does provide a richer understanding of textual functions, but presumes the arrival of the text at a prompt instant between production and audiencing. Emphasizing the ways in which the social audience is shaped, in both Gramscian hegemonic and Habermasian public sphere variants, by the constraints that production and public discourse place on it, the cultural studies tradition has likewise rarely addressed distribution, the determining instanced that what is not available cannot be contested, and that control over what is distributed determines the grounds on which contestation can occur. In Stuart Hall's (1997) cyclical model, the key networked terms are representation, identity, production, regulation and consumption. Regulation here impacts on production, mediates between representation and consumption, and articulates with identity. But regulation is not only a matter of policy or cultural bylaws. It is the positive activity of managing territories, deferring arrivals and articulating agencies within as well as without the media industries. Given the centrality of lived audiences to cultural studies, of textuality to hermeneutics, and engineering standards to information theory, the lack of address to distribution is understandable. A media-based analysis of media cannot however afford this lacuna. The most convincing contemporary political economist of the media, Vincent Mosco (1996) deploys categories of commodification, spatialization and structuration as a basis for analyzing relations between economic and political cycles of media. His analysis is processual, describing activities that occur throughout the media cycle but which come to a sharp focus in the distributive moment.

Unlike theoretical writers, historical analyses of major industries such as film (Gomery 1992; Wasko 2003), radio (Barnouw 1966), television (Boddy 1993) and popular music (Sanjek and Sanjek 1991; Burnett 1996), and more specialized studies like Oliver Boyd-Barrett's of *The International News Agencies* (1980), do foreground issues of distribution. The distribution of ideas outside the industrial media are the subject of key work by Appadurai (1996) and Hannerz (1996) among many other scholars of globalization. That this perspective should become available in the opening years of the twenty-first century is itself a product of the cultural politics of the network society, and particularly of the growing centrality of IP to contemporary capital and to neoliberal globalization strategies. Castells, from whom the term derives, distinguishes three features of the network society:

- it is *informational*: knowledge generation and information management determine the productivity and competitiveness of firms, industries, regions

- it is *global*: "its core strategic activities have the capacity to work as a unit on a planetary scale in real time or chosen time" (Castells 2000: 10)
- it is *networked*: it is premised on "the Internet-based, interactive, networked connection between producers, consumers and service providers" (Castells 2001: 75)

This analysis, revisited with the focus on mediation, devolves not on the geographical optic of the "space of flows," but on the production of IP and its management as more than a rapidly growing sector of the economy (IIPA figures show growth of US copyright industries from $178.8 billion in 1977, to $765.6 billion in 2000, and to $791.2 billion in 2001 [IIPA 2002: 17]). They also provide the model for any successful enterprise. The management of IP, the ability to share knowledge and its management globally, and the networked interactivity of all participants in the network economy, in short all three of Castells' categories of network society, belong to the activity here described as distribution.

The materiality of distribution's role is underlined in Article 2 of the World Intellectual Property Organization (WIPO) Copyright Treaty: "Copyright protection extends to expressions and not to ideas, procedures, methods of operation or mathematical concepts as such" (WIPO 1996). An idea is not intellectual property until it is expressed in a material form – that is until it becomes available for distribution. This in turn implies the existence of physical infrastructures through which content can reach audiences. James Wilsdon notes another aspect of the materiality of IP distribution, again involving business-to-business (B2B) trade:

> Back in July [2000], Amazon.com teamed up with Federal Express to deliver 250,000 copies of the new Harry Potter book to eager US fans. True to the spirit of 1–click™ shopping, no effort was spared in ensuring that the book hit people's doormats on the morning of publication. A press release issued the next day proudly declared it to be "one of the largest sales and distribution events in e-commerce history". In just 24 hours, over 300 tonnes or 188 million pages of Harry Potter magic were transported to homes across America... At strategic locations across America, a fleet of 9000 trucks revved their engines, 100 planes rolled down the runways. Their mission: to deliver *Harry Potter and the Goblet of Fire* to a nation hungry for instant fulfilment.

The distribution of the physical objects that producers make is big business – with a measurable environmental impact. And each element of the infrastructure from conduits to contracts is a potential node at which "value" can be produced, or exchange-value extracted. Agencies that specialize in getting programers in front of schedulers, authors' and actors' agents, CD and DVD design and pressing plants, retailers and point-of-sale advertising, all participate, and all regulate, the traffic between makers and meanings. Anyone can make a song or a story, but getting songs and stories out to the public is a specialist, strategic exercise. Keeping information and ideas out of public circulation is equally a function of distribution. Both promoting and denying circulation confer wealth and power, introducing disjunctures, deferrals, omissions and selections that restructure and reorganize both content and audience activity.

DISTRIBUTION INDUSTRIES

Even in industrial circles where distribution is understood as a clearly separate activity from production, there can be difficulties establishing its boundaries. In many media, distribution companies belong to producers as in the case of Disney's Buena Vista wing (Wasko 2001: 42–8) and the global film distributor United International Pictures, whose major shareholders are Paramount (Viacom) and MGM-UA (now Sony and Comcast; Acland 2003: 31 cites figures suggesting that twelve distributors control 96 percent of global film traffic). Pricing in the entertainment industries – the actualization of exchange-value – bewilders the most ardent economists: from the agent-regulated supply of stars' appearances to the marginal cost of selling a TV show to a developing-world network. Even in relatively straightforward exchanges like those between distributors and theatre owners, complex contracts regulate such aspects as ticket prices, the number of screens showing a film, the number of shows per day and the duration of the run. And even a wholly owned subsidiary like Buena Vista can evolve its own priorities and tactics vis-à-vis its proprietor and its sister theater chain over a period of years. So for example *Broadcasting & Cable* reported on Feb 4, 2002, "AOL Time Warner nets The WB, TNT and TBS Superstation will pony up at least $75 million for New Line Cinema's *Lord of the Rings: The Fellowship of the Ring* and two upcoming sequels," observing that New Line as well as the three cable stations are all AOL-Time-Warner subsidiaries. Transfer pricing involved in global exchanges deploys the spatial differences between information values in yet more complex ways. The accounting procedures – and the significant revenue streams derived from them – involved in this trade would require a separate specialist study, but the impact of differential pricing across space and time clearly impacts on the free flow of communication.

Time also plays a role in the interaction between distributors and producers in the form of feed-forward loops. Independent exhibitors and international distributors competing for a blockbuster movie will enter into contracts with producers that may be signed before a single camera rolls. Toy and fast-food franchises gamble on the success of the film, influencing its composition (perhaps through product placement for example) but also sign up to restrictions on how images and themes can be used. Producers, exhibitors and purchasers can be legally bound to use the product in restricted ways, exemplified in the copyright warnings at the beginning of every DVD and VHS. Distribution benefits and binds all parties. Equally, all parties within and without the industry are engaged in complex chains of payment and credit that can become extremely fraught. In return for a slice of their earnings, talent agencies like MCA and William Morris (Rose 1995) regulate the availability of stars, directors and scriptwriters among others, with notoriously tangled financial and contractual procedures. B2B deals can be equally constraining, as was the case, notoriously, with Technicolor contracts in the 1930s and 1940s that required the company's technicians to be on set throughout, promoting the interests of the process at times in opposition to those of the film's director of photography and director. Joint ventures and strategic alliances require fiercely complex accounting and legal structures. The internal and external dynamics of distribution then include massive internal redistribution of content, data and money, not a simple two-way flow of money in exchange for content.

Distributors like UIP and Buena Vista are responsible for bringing the revenues from audiences back through the chain to the producers. Large corporations like UK-based advertising giant WPP charge for a range of services including media buying for marketing campaigns, market research, hard- and software delivery and accounting, all of which require credit and other banking services charged back to other divisions, thence to the client and ultimately to their consumers. The strategic position of film distributors between the box-office and the studio, to take a familiar example, requires meticulous oversight and skilled accounting, not least because figures have to be presented one way for studio heads and another for bankers, a third way for talent and differently again for advertising purposes. As movement of money on national and global scales becomes increasingly electronic, the distinction between the directions of flow diminishes, for example as presales of miscellaneous distribution rights become significant parts of production financing (Caves 2000: 161–71). In the case of film distribution, a physical product still has to arrive at a cinema, and in older times cash had to change hands. But now that product can be delivered and revenues handled electronically, the position of distribution as the nexus through which digital signals flow in both directions is clearer than in the analog/photomechanical period. Distributors derive rents from the media they handle, including financial media. These rents arise from control over flows: delaying a release here in order to boost the prestige and prices of a premiere there, charging higher for the freshest news and therefore delaying its arrival to lower-paying users, speeding up or slowing down returns from consumers to the various service providers involved in the distribution process. Talent who opt to take points or royalties may wait considerably longer than investors, frequently companies like HBO whose core business is distribution, who have extended credit to a production and who are therefore charging interest. Distribution is then not only a question of geography but also of time.

Refining the initial definition then, distribution can be considered as the management of space-time flows of product and money. There is also an informational aspect to distribution. Not only does distribution bring news, entertainment and advertising to audiences; it is also a feedback loop. The cash flow returning to producers is not merely money: it is also vital data confirming the performance of products in the marketplace, and thereby shaping both the future handling of the current product and what further products will be commissioned. Box-office statistics, like pop-music charts, are significant elements in marketing and in the management of creative industry careers. In this sense, the television-ratings business belongs to the distributive moment of the media cycle. Moreover, not only absolute but also relative returns signify. Absolute numbers can fluctuate as whole markets rise and fall seasonally (for example around Christmas) and across larger scales (such as the fall in cinema attendance associated with the arrival of video and its rise in the age of the multiplex [Acland 2003]). The relative success of Disney and AOL-Time-Warner is also of significance to shareholders and industry observers, who in turn distribute information on market share and reach to potential advertisers or partners in the lucrative spin-off markets like fast-food, clothing and computer games (Doyle 2002).

Wherever the point of sale, a new industry derives further profit not just from the money that changes hands, but also from data associated with the exchange (Gandy 1993). A credit card transaction for a barcoded ticket locates a purchaser at a specific outlet at a specific time, and matches the purchase with a profile of other purchases to produce data sets that can be sold on to marketing agencies and ultimately back to producers. Loyalty cards in physical stores and cookies in online sales environments harvest data, much of it culled without the buyers' knowledge. Other information is amassed through the use of phone-ins, especially those using mobile phones, competitions and prize-draw questionnaires. Whether this data-gathering is a genuine exchange (Dyson 1997) or a near-fraudulent purloining (Elmer 2004), it constitutes a major element of the value of the act of purchasing, combining money flows with information flows that return through the distribution chain to be amassed among corporate conglomerates as a tool for gaining market advantage and militating against start-up companies seeking access to the industry. Once again, money and data are decreasingly distinguishable.

Technologies themselves require distribution, the more so since the media cycle depends on audiences supplying their own tools, tools that the media industries must bring to markets where they can be purchased. Transport is also critical to the movement of people, who themselves constitute media when they are the vehicles for distributing songs, jokes, religious rituals, languages and other communications, the most vital for cinema being word-of-mouth publicity. Long considered integral to the sociology and geography of communications, transport becomes only more clearly integrated into media communication when not only container loads of TV sets but also satellite delivery of hundreds of channels of audiovisual, telecoms and data are added to global trade, and as financial flows integrate telecoms with the trade in goods and services. Transport is one of the tools available to distribution for rationing media. The relative speeds of airfreight, seafreight, land transport can affect not just the delivery of film prints but also of documents, contracts and bank drafts, customs clearances and carnets, delaying or accelerating the arrival of hardware and software in global markets differentiated by their proximity or distance, measured in weeks rather than miles, from the centers of the media industry. Levies can be raised at every level from the costs of import policy change to corruption among functionaries

One further sectoral interest in distribution remains to note: the role of the state. Though nation states have lost much of their economic and political autonomy in the era of globalization, and indeed perhaps as a direct result of that loss, governments have devoted a great deal of energy to maintaining a stake in the control of information and entertainment (see for example the interventionist ethos of the UK's Creative Industries Task Force report on television export markets, Department for Culture, Media and Sport 1998). Censorship, state-run media, industry regulation and tariffs have been used to limit the permeability of given states to both free markets and alternative media. More positively, many countries provide substantial subsidies to public service media, and to cultural sectors including minority languages and culturally validated forms like cinema, opera, theater and dance. The most staunchly protectionist market is undoubtedly the United States, which has developed idiosyncratic technical standards (for example in television and cellphone telecoms) as well as corporate strategies that help exclude the country from global media product (Herman and McChesney 1997; Wasko 2003: 80 gives figures of domestic box-office take for Hollywood studios and their affiliates of 80–90 percent). The engagement of states in distribution is thus both positive and negative, both promoting specific production sectors and limiting others. As generators of information, governments also seek to control their own media flows through selective leaks and schedules for press and media releases. Censorship traditionally meant the geographical control of information. Given the leakiness of electronic media, designed both to transmit and copy, censorship now tends toward the temporal control of delay. In many instances, the result is the same: what might have been a shocking revelation on the day is a mere historical footnote a matter of weeks or even days later. Like any human activity, governance cannot but communicate. Nations' role in distribution is shaped by the same priorities as corporations': promoting some flows and delaying or denying others, where possible amassing monopoly use of key data, and struggling to maintain both the monopoly and the legitimations for it.

THE WORK OF DISTRIBUTION

For the workforce in the distribution sector, the amount of work required to deliver product to audiences, and revenues and data to producers, cannot be underestimated. Film distributors, for example, do far more than dump movies in cinemas, though that is itself a massive transport effort when opening weekends may see up to three or four thousand prints delivered in the USA alone. Apart from the provision of security against piracy, in the expanded realm of electronic distribution distributors not only handle promotion but also new media formats, whose standing hinges on their ability to match users to products, and on their creditworthiness with suppliers. This gives the distributor the advantage of being able to recommend specific product lines, but makes them vulnerable to major suppliers seeking to maintain or challenge market dominance, and diminishes the incentives to pioneer new hardware and software formats. Thus distributors must mediate between the rival claims of homeostasis and change in the consumer end of their business, where change will involve the development of new and the gradual decay of established markets and product lines. Radical innovation involves the creation of a new audience, defined by its embrace of the new product. Routine novelty maintains and reaffirms an existing audience construction. In either case, the information content of distribution involves either space or time or both: an established product to a new market (Hollywood film in the People's Republic), or a new product in an established market (DVD usurping VHS). Innovation is measurable as a ratio between the expected and the unexpected, with zero information content at either end of the spectrum (repetition or noise). But this ratio is not absolute, as long as it depends on what is predictable in a given geographical zone. Giant cable distributor HBO, for example, has established a major reputation for quality drama, using one successful innovation (*The Sopranos*) to launch others (such as *Six Feet Under*) where the ninety–minute, adult-themed, idiosyncratic series drama has become a recognizable genre of its own. Entrusted with supplying producers with information about what is likely to succeed in future based on their experience of what has succeeded in the recent past, distributors must balance the claims of formula and familiarity against the need for constant novelty. Their considerable expertise in regional and sectoral variation, which they can sell back to producers, provides distributors with another profit stream. In this way distribution mediates between the space-time parameters of media on the one hand, and information about their reception on the other. Such information takes the form of money returned from paying customers as well as data about their preferences, both circulated in the form of electronic data streams. Thus a key task of distribution is to ensure the redistribution of money in space and time.

Information itself has monetary value. It must be timely to be information at all, and must be delivered to geographically specific audiences. These audiences are constructed in hierarchies. Thus distributors will often provide key reviewers, retailers and increasingly influential fansites with advance access to restricted previews and trade shows in order to create prerelease buzz. In exchange, such access underwrites the industry kudos of key distributive functionaries in radio stations, press and rental chains. A similar service is provided by film festivals like Cannes, industry conferences like SIGGRAPH (the premier event for computer graphics professionals) and markets like the Frankfurt Book Fair, even academic conferences. Attendance marks attendees as players, and in return attendees act as conduits for new product and product lines to their home markets with the increased mana derived from their involvement. The real targets of such restricted events are always at one remove, both spatially and temporally; not so much the tastemaker as her circle of influence. To be "where it's at" implies being there before the mass market arrives, at a distinct place and a distinct moment. The delay between expert and mass distribution is a crucial one in terms of the production of value, social, financial and informational. These restrictions of media flows to specific audiences at specific times indicate a key task of distribution: participation in the construction of audiences. Professional audiences (such as members of the Academy of Motion Picture Arts and Sciences) are more valuable than commercially or politically distinguished audiences (women, youth, etc.), and these more than nonspecific audiences that must make up in numbers what they lack in specialization.

The value of information diminishes not solely according to time but in direct proportion to the attention that it generates. Media retailers, including not only broadcasters but also cinema operators, video store and bookshop managers and newsagents, are paid for delivering audiences.[3] Making sure that key audiences see the right media at the right time is a skilled profession. Tastemakers must get sneak previews, but release must be delayed. Fear of piracy now favors global simultaneous release for entertainment media, but even simultaneity requires carefully restricted press previews and security at laboratories, studios and manufacturing plants. Software beta testing demands a wide and expert user base, but also restriction to that base in advance of full public release. In this context, media crime is a levy on a levy. Stolen media and communications hardware and their resale constitute a significant part of the grey economy. Systems and technologies designed to make theft and resale more difficult also form part of the distributive cycle. The same is true of fraud, IP and data theft and of attempts to stem them. The mutual surveillance of criminals and security experts is significant work, and therefore also a significant source of profit and power. It should be clear however that the vast majority of hard- and software crime, despite the emotive epithet "organised," is undertaken without institutional organization parallel to the scale of, say, News Corp. Criminal redistribution of hardware suffers especially from the lack of organized transportation; IP theft lacks the organizational impact of data sets held by entertainment cartels or monopoly suppliers of news like government information agencies; and both lack that organization which creates valuably disciplined audiences.

As Stiglitz (2002) observes, classical economics presumes ideally informed consumers, but where the market is itself a market in information, then stockpiling, delaying and selective releasing of information constructs the market as unequal, a fact enshrined in the secrecy with which national, corporate and global organizations like the IMF conduct their business. These inequalities arise in the mediations that distribution performs in distributing stasis and change across space and time, in the process differentiating the public into market segments distinguished by their degrees of specialized consumption skills, strategic redistributive positions and the complexity of the data they produce as well as the disposable income they command. Constituting a market segment as gendered or as national, for example, is achieved by selective releasing and withholding of information, emphasizing human interest stories in one market, withholding overseas news in the other. From guild membership to the early adopter lifestyle group, valuable markets are constructed in the formation of mediascapes undertaken in the distributive feedback loops of mediation. Current innovations like viral marketing into playgrounds indicate the levels at which these processes are colonizing even the regulated spaces of childhood.

THEORY AND PRACTICE OF DISTRIBUTION

What politics there may be, what culture may come about in the twenty-first century will be mediated. In existing democracies not only is voting a mediated form but voters are also represented, their views garnered as polls and referendums and mediated as statistical aggregations. Their politicians engage in public relations via print and electronic media, political decisions are mediated as laws, demonstrators perform for city streets and terrorists for the mass media. The media itself is thoroughly mediated in national lobbies, in international policy forums like IIPA and the International Telecommunications Union's World Summit on the Information Society (WSIS), and in international treaties like WIPO and Trade in Intellectual Property and Services (TRIPS) addendum to the WTO treaty. At the same time, civil movements have embraced new technologies of networked and mobile media. The crucial difference between corporate mass media and citizens' media is neither the skill with which they are constructed nor the ability to elicit passionate commitment from audiences. It lies instead in the challenge of getting messages to audiences, in short in the field of distribution. The processes of getting stories and slogans out to the wider public, and especially the challenge of matching the global reach of increasingly convergent infotainment, computing and telecommunications corporations, requires the development of alternative channels of distribution.

Undertaken locally and globally by religions, diasporas, families, friendship networks, voluntary organizations and fan cultures, "cultural" distribution nets overlay the "market" systems of mass media, sometimes amplifying class, race and gender segmentation, sometimes muting them. This distributed form of distribution may involve reinforcements of tradition, locality, identity as well as challenges to and innovations in them, in aggregate resonating with Rosenau's (2003) "fragmegration." Alternative mediations, it is true, always run the risk of becoming the unpaid research and development wings of corporate capital, but only so long as they are dependent on corporate means of distribution. Establishing alternate circuits of dialogue, and the constant reinvention of distributive mechanisms as a tactic for avoiding co-option, are a central plank of distributive politics and distributive ethics. Their association with criminality in officially circulated media – for example the illegal transport of migrants, the specter of hacking, and the association of alternative media with terrorism – is an indication of the extremism with which privileged access to the means of distribution is protected.

Certain kinds of information are only valuable if they are not distributed. Military secrets, police evidence (especially during investigations) and the workings of central banks are examples of information that gains in value to the extent that it is withheld from distribution. This negative distribution is itself a function of the distributive moment, and generates both wealth and power. Theft, for example, requires secrecy for success. The more people involved in a crime, the more important the distribution of information becomes. High-risk crimes like confidence tricks require a carefully managed distribution of partial information and disinformation, a careful balancing of fiction and fact, to secure their goals. The restriction of information to professional groups is considered a legitimate cost of efficiency, even of democracy: budgets are not released preferentially, jury deliberations are protected from undue scrutiny, and armed forces routinely withhold information. There are certainly ethical issues involved here (Where is the threshold between legitimate concealment of privileged discussions and illegitimate concealment of covert actions?). Ethics in distribution can be read as an economics of power and a politics of the economic.

Professional and philosophical ethics here concern the legitimacy or otherwise of control over the positive and negative distribution of information. Negative distribution includes, for example, withholding a consumer profile from the consumer, restricting access to audience information for the audience surveyed, and restricting the design of market research in the interests of corporate goals. Positive distribution includes the dissemination of professional ethics and codes of practice. Both contribute to a core function of distribution: the process of legitimating the differential treatment of mediation across its dimensional and informational modes. If "Social systems can be viewed as networks of communicative actions; personality systems can be regarded under the aspect of the ability to speak and act" (Habermas 1979: 98), the distributed nature of these networks and abilities intervenes in the processes whereby the accumulation of mediation is acceptable or contested. Acceptance and contestation in their turn need to be mediated and therefore distributed, under the systemic conditions examined here of accelerations, deferrals and selections. The "ability to speak" requires, for its realization, access to someone to speak to.

All human communication requires its moment of address. In dialogic communities we can still hear the mutuality of that relationship in call-and-response patterns. Even at this innocent level, however, audiences do not constitute themselves. Nor are they constructed by textuality or by technologies. The art of directing communication to the people who will want it is now the science of market segmentation. The construction of the other as other is a moment of communication that divides by directing communications preferentially and reserving some communications for peers alone. Typically, this results in ascribing to those excluded from communications an inability to communicate. This discrimination has been raised to a science in contemporary distribution, underpinned by a history of control over mediations that has produced those inequalities, expropriations and antagonisms on which the dark contradictions of the commodity form have arisen. Despite the characterization of globalization as "powerless places and placeless power," media systems still operate on a deeply conservative maintenance of spatial relations. Ex-colonial capitals still have significant impact on the distributive systems of their old colonies (see for example Armes 1985), and the system linking Southern California to the East Coast banks established in the 1910s (Wasko 1986) remains hegemonic. This geographic specificity distinguishes distribution in the globalization process, an indicator of its potential for blocking the evolution of human communication.

Other modes of distribution exist. Indigenous rights based on community, tradition, trust and intimacy are antipathetic to the legal "persons," almost exclusively corporations, who own IP and dominate global treaty making (Yudice 2003: 218–21). Others are based on democracy and many-to-many technologies, and integrate with projects to build alternative audiences. Their development is likely to be the subject of papers in this journal. Meanwhile every stage of commodity distribution is prone to mishaps. Backfiring projects and criminal actions disenable any attempt to erect a watertight system for controlling what is by its nature the infinitely fecund generation of human communications. Globalization brings not only localization but also alternative modes of global relationships, from crime syndicates to diasporas, which act as distributive networks, outside the whale as well as inside. The development of P2P (peer-to-peer) networks, of Open Source software (and its recent adoption by the UN: see http://www.iosn.org/), the economics of barter implied by the Creative

Commons movement all point to alternative modes of distribution to place alongside informal community television, video workshops and small label music networks.

Resistance is a property of the strong. For too long media and cultural studies have posited resistance as a code word for positive values – resistant texts, cultures and readings have marked the good in disciplines that eschew the intrinsic values of connoisseurship. From the systemic perspective of mediation theory, resistance is a restriction of flow. For a politics that believes that wealth and power originate with the wealthy and powerful, a politics of resistance makes sense. But if, as mediation theory proposes, it is the land (Leopold 2001), the multitudes (Hardt and Negri 2000) and the history of the species stored in technologies and techniques that is creative and productive, then resistance is the role of the oppressor. As the sources of wealth lie in human, natural and fixed capital, so the sources of power lie in the same upwellings from below. Political power and accumulated wealth derive from these, characteristically from blocking, deferring, redirecting, levying and stockpiling flow: in short, from resisting the open system. The disenfranchised always demand change. The wealthy and entrenched always seek ways to stop it. Even when they claim to innovate, or urge the demands of a new class fraction among the rulers, they always pursue stagnation of the fundamental division of society into those with access to information, money and power, and those without. The oppressed are not powerless but the source of power, the creators of wealth even though they are poor. The rich want our power and our wealth. The ideology of resistance reverses the real relations of emergence and stasis, ascribing stasis to those from whom communication flows, and emergence to those whose power and wealth derives from blocking it. The politics of resistance is a kind of benevolent populist conservatism: the rich instructing the poor on how to resist change, when change is invariably in the interests of those who suffer. We should not instruct our students that taking over the existing institutions is worthless: systemic change is at least as likely to come incrementally as by revolution. But we have no business telling them that they should be resistant. Far more important to create new circuits, new economies, alongside the new technologies and techniques that are such a hallmark of the contemporary mediascape. Analysis of distribution is the key to liberating communication in the twenty-first century.

NOTES

The author would like to acknowledge the advice and input of Bill MacArthur and the painstaking reviewers of *Cultural Politics*.

1. The work of audiencing, of disciplined and differentiated attention, produces the significance that the raw objects made in production do not possess. Significance is equally a matter of meanings, of

numbers, of reaching target audiences, and of the information audiences generate in the acts of purchasing and interacting with the media. To the extent that capitalism measures significance as value, it is the quantum of audience attention that is traded in industrial media, though corporate data acquisition systems and holdings are increasingly accounted as assets.

2. In the current analysis, technologies belong properly to the production moment of the media cycle. Technologies give form (dimensionality) to the physical attributes of media, and concurrently actualize (give physical presence to) the dimensions of space and time as they are constructed in media. The product of production is thus an object, physically constituted in space and time, an essential element of the process of creating commodities. This mediation is then further mediated in distribution. McLuhan (for example 1964), like apparatus theory (see Heath and de Lauretis 1980), does not look in detail at delivery mechanisms beyond the space-time determinations of the object, inferring that the object, in this instance the technologies used to convey content, also produces effects in the audience, demeaning the audiences' work on the media. To the extent that hardware is integral to the experience of most media, and that broadcast, for example, is experienced differently to the reading of a book, McLuhan's observations are correct. But the relative invisibility of the distributive moment implies that technologies are not always experienced by audiences at all, as with data harvesting or freight. Nor is the cycle of media exclusively determined by either the content (the messages of information theory) or the technologies of production.

3. End users are not only active audiences, participating in the production of meaning: they also work – again, unpaid – on the distribution of media, in the household, in gift giving, in small public spaces like bars where the choice of certain kinds of music or certain types of television program are channeled preferentially into micromarkets that gradually take interest in the media which are supposed to interest them (capital's market variant on Lacan's *sujet supposé savoir*). This is a part of the process of consumer discipline – the construction of common media interests that consequently define specific age cohorts, class fractions, sexualities and lifestyle groups.

REFERENCES

Acland, Charles R. 2003. *Screen Traffic: Movies, Multiplexes and Global Culture*. Durham: Duke University Press.

Albarran, Alan B. 2002. *Media Economics: Understanding Markets, Industries and Concepts*. 2nd edn., Ames: Iowa State Press.

Appadurai, Arjun. 1996. *Modernity at Large: Cultural Dimensions of Globalization*. Minneapolis: University of Minnesota Press.

Armes, Roy. 1985. "Black African Cinema in the Eighties." *Screen*, 26(3–4), May-August.

Barnouw, Eric. 1966. *A Tower in Babel: A History of Broadcasting in the United States: Volume 1 to 1933*. New York: Oxford University Press.

—— 1982. *Tube of Plenty: The Evolution of American Television*. Rev. edn. New York: Oxford University Press.

Boddy, William. 1993. *Fifties Television: The Industry and Its Critics*. Urbana: Indiana University Press.

Boyd-Barrett, Oliver. 1980. *The International News Agencies*. London: Constable.

Burnett, Robert. 1996. *The Global Jukebox: The International Music Industry*. London: Routledge.

Castells, Manuel. 1996. *The Information Age: Economy, Society and Culture Volume One, The Rise of the Network Society*. Oxford: Blackwell.

—— 2000. "Materials for an Exploratory Theory of the Network Society." *British Journal of Sociology*, 51(1): 5–24.

—— 2001. *The Internet Galaxy: Reflections on the Internet, Business and Society*. Oxford: Oxford University Press.

Caves, Richard E. 2000. *Creative Industries: Contracts Between Art and Commerce*. Cambridge: Harvard University Press.

Department for Culture, Media and Sport. 1998. *Creative Industries UK Television Exports Inquiry: The Report of the Creative Industries Task Force Inquiry into Television Exports*. London: Department for Culture, Media and Sport.

Douglas, Susan J. 1987. *Inventing American Broadcasting 1899–1922*. Baltimore: Johns Hopkins University Press.

Doyle, Gillian. 2002. *Understanding Media Economics*. London: Sage.

Dyson, Esther. 1997. *Release 2.0: A Design for Living in the Digital Age*. New York: Viking.

Economist. 2004. "MGM and Sony: Into the Sunset." 18–24 September, p. 68.

Elmer, Greg. 2004. *Profiling Machines: Mapping the Personal Information Economy*. Cambridge: MIT Press.

Fischer, Claude S. 1992. *America Calling: A Social History of the Telephone to 1940*. Baltimore: Johns Hopkins University Press.

Gandy, Oscar H. Jnr. 1993. *The Panoptic Sort: The Political Economy of Personal Information*. Boulder: Westview Press.

Gomery, Douglas. 1986. *The Hollywood Studio System*. London: BFI Macmillan.

—— 1992. *Shared Pleasures: A History of Movie Presentation in the United States*. London: BFI.

Habermas, Jürgen. 1979. *Communication and the Evolution of Society*. Trans. Thomas McCarthy. London: Heineman.

—— 1993. *Moral Consciousness and Communicative Action*. Trans. Christian Lenhardt and Shierry Weber Nicholson. Cambridge: MIT Press.

Hall, Stuart (ed.). 1997. *Representation: Cultural Representations and Signifying Practices*. London: Sage.

Hannerz, Ulf. 1996. *Transnational Connections: Culture, People, Places*. London: Routledge.

Hardt, Michael and Negri, Antonio. 2000. *Empire*. Cambridge: Harvard University Press.

Heath, Stephen and de Lauretis, Theresa. (eds). 1980. *The Cinematic Apparatus*. London: Macmillan.

Herman, Edward S. and McChesney, Robert W. 1997. *The Global Media: The New Missionaries of Corporate Capitalism*. New York: Continuum.

IIPA (International Intellectual Property Alliance. 2002. *Copyright Industries in the U.S. Economy: The 2002 Report*. Prepared by Stephen E. Siwek, Economists Incorporated. Washington DC: IIPA.

Kieve, Jeffrey. 1973. *The Electric Telegraph in the U.K.: A Social and Economic History*. Newton Abbott: David and Charles.

Klein, Naomi. 2000. *No Logo: Taking Aim at the Brand Bullies*. London: Flamingo.

Lardner, James. 1987. *Fast Forward: Hollywood, the Japanese and the VCR Wars*. New York: Mentor.

Leopold, Aldo. 2001. "Ecocentrism: The Land Ethic." In Louis P. Pojman (ed.), *Environmental Ethics: Readings in Theory and Application*. Belmont: Wadsworth, pp. 119–26.

McLuhan, Marshall. 1964. *Understanding Media: The Extensions of Man*. London: Sphere.

Marx, Karl. 1973. *Grundrisse*. Trans. Martin Nicolaus. London: Penguin/New Left Books.

—— 1976. *Capital: A Critique of Political Economy*. Vol. 1, trans. Rodney Livingstone. London: NLB/Penguin.

Mosco, Vincent. 1996. *The Political Economy of Communication: Rethinking and Renewal*. London: Sage.

Rose, Frank. 1995. *The Agency: William Morris and the Hidden History of Show Business*. New York: Harper Collins.

Rosenau, James N. 2003. *Distant Proximities: Dynamics Beyond Globalization*. Princeton: Princeton University Press.

Sanjek, Russell, and Sanjek, David. 1991. *American Popular Music Business in the 20th Century*. Oxford: Oxford University Press.

Schatz, Thomas. 1981. *Hollywood Genres: Formulas, Filmmaking and the Studio System*. New York: Random House.

Schiller, Dan. 1999. *Digital Capitalism: Networking the Global Marketing System*. Cambridge: MIT Press.

Smith, Anthony (ed.) 1995. *Television: An International History*. Oxford: Oxford University Press.

Smythe, Dallas. 1994. "Communications: Blindspot of Western Marxism [1977]." In *Counterclockwise: Perspectives on Communication*, ed. Thomas Guback. Boulder: Westview Press, pp. 266–91; originally published in *Canadian Journal of Political and Social Theory*, 1(3), Fall 1977: 1–27.

Stiglitz, Joseph. 2002. *Globalization and its Discontents*. London: Penguin.

Wasko, Janet. 1986. "DW Griffith and the Banks: A Case Study in Film Financing." In Paul Kerr (ed.), *The Hollywood Film Industry*, London: BFI, pp. 31–42.

—— 2001. *Understanding Disney*. Cambridge: Polity.

—— 2003. *How Hollywood Works*. Thousand Oaks: Sage.

Wilsdon, James. 2001. *dot-com ethics: e-business & sustainability*. London: Digital Futures.

WIPO (World Intellectual Property Organisation) 1996. *WIPO Copyright Treaty and Agreed Statements Concerning the WIPO Copyright Treaty*. Adopted in Geneva on December 20, 1996.

Yudicé, George. 2003. *The Expediency of Culture: Uses of Culture in the Global Era*. Durham: Duke University Press.

CULTURAL POLITICS   VOLUME 1, ISSUE 2   PP 215–232

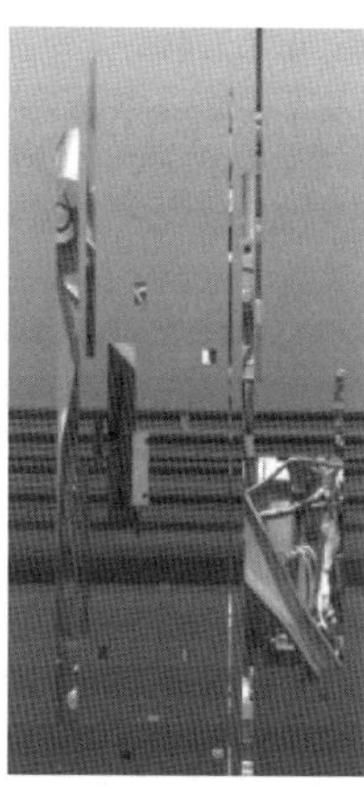

LUCK, POWER, CORRUPTION, DEMOCRACY? JUDGING ARTS PRIZES

JOHN STREET

JOHN STREET TEACHES POLITICS AT THE UNIVERSITY OF EAST ANGLIA. HE IS THE AUTHOR OF SEVERAL BOOKS, INCLUDING *POLITICS AND POPULAR CULTURE* (POLITY 1997) AND *MASS MEDIA, POLITICS AND DEMOCRACY* (PALGRAVE 2001).

ABSTRACT   Arts prizes have become an increasingly prominent part of the cultural landscape, influencing not only the careers of individual artists but also the policies of cultural industries and cultural institutions. Despite this, relatively little detailed attention has been given to the arts prize. While at the same time media-generated conventional wisdom has tended to portray prize juries as acting either corruptly or irrationally. This article challenges such views, and argues that the prize jury needs to be understood as a form of political institution, in which decision rules, power and other factors play their part. This conclusion is reached through the detailed study of three UK arts prizes.

INTRODUCTION

Reporting on the dinner given for the winner of the UK's Booker Prize for literature, the journalist David Robson wrote:

Of course, the whole thing is the most colossal confidence trick. There is a race and a winner and the winner gets a prize. But there are no rules – and the audience know there are no rules. The illusion, intrinsic to the process, that there are sophisticated judging procedures from which the year's best novel emerges, can only be sustained by a superhuman willingness to suspend one's disbelief' (*Sunday Telegraph*, November 12, 1995).

Another journalist wrote of the UK and Ireland's Mercury Music Prize: "The judges will pick a name out of the hat, safe in the knowledge that no one could argue logically whether the choice they've made is the right one or the wrong one" (Nicholas Barber, *Independent on Sunday*, September 5, 1999). This is a common view. Arts prizes are often portrayed as an elaborate exercise in trickery or mythmaking. It is a view not confined to journalists, but shared by the competitors themselves. The novelist Martin Amis (2000: 46) likens the literary prize to a lottery: "Writers become something you can bet on, and when lottery-night comes round you can watch them on TV being reduced to what Yiddish calls *schwitzers* – stealthily perspiring into their tuxes." Another author, Julian Barnes, describes the literary award as "a posh form of bingo" (Burn 1987: 38). Or as the writer and television presenter Melvyn Bragg commented: "It is clearly barking mad to attempt final judgments on paintings, songs, books or anything artistic that moves" (*The Times*, October 13, 1997). The widespread perception of arts prizes as arbitrary and irrational might count for little if the prizes were themselves of no significance, but it can be argued that they matter a great deal.

Not only have they proliferated in recent years, distributing large quantities of cash to the winners, but they have also had a major impact on the market for cultural goods, turning authors, musicians and artists into household names, boosting their sales by several hundred percent. They also affect routine practices within the public and private sector, shaping what kind of work is commissioned or subsidized. Writing of the impact of piano competitions, Charles Rosen (2002: 110) suggests: "a student who wins a prize is most often viewed as a vindication of the method of instruction or of the school." Prizes assume a wider importance as representative – particularly through the role of sponsorship – of the commodification and commercialization of art. And finally, prizes can matter for the way they shape popular taste and sensibilities by legitimating cultural forms and expressions (see Street 2002, for a fuller review of the consequences of arts prizes).

Despite these arguments for taking arts prizes seriously, remarkably little has been written on the topic (for exceptions, see Goff 1989; Todd 1996). This is partly a consequence of the secrecy that protects jury deliberations. It is also a consequence of the fact that arts prizes, in so far as they have been acknowledged, have been located in the general context of cultural policy and economics (e.g. Caves 2000: 196–9). This article is, therefore, an attempt to focus attention on the contemporary arts prize, and in particular on the process of judging. It asks whether arts prize juries are, in fact, the equivalent of a random number generator. It draws on research into three annual UK-based arts prizes: the Booker Prize for literature (worth £50,000 and awarded to a British and Commonwealth novel); the Whitbread Book of the Year award (worth £30,000 and awarded to a British book from a variety of genres – poetry, fiction, children's literature and non-fiction); and the Mercury Music Prize (worth £20,000 and awarded to the best album made by a British or Irish artist). This is a small selection of the many prizes awarded each year, but they are among the most prominent in the UK. And for the purposes of the research reported here they stand as "typical" of the general process of reaching a decision about which work of culture should win the prize. The research itself, which began in 2000, is based on interviews with arts prize judges and chairs of juries, as well as with prize organizers. It has also made extensive use of archival and contemporary records.[1]

This article concentrates on the process of judging these prizes. It challenges the view that the awarding of prizes is a random or irrational process, and argues instead that it is a political one. Prize jury deliberation and decision making parallel processes familiar to students of politics. They are affected by the application of particular decision rules, by the distribution of power and by the ideals that inform behavior. To draw attention to the cultural politics of arts prizes is, therefore, to establish a quite different perception of them. This is important not only for our understanding of prizes themselves but also for wider debates about the operation of esthetic judgement more generally.

LUCK, REASON OR CORRUPTION?

Conventional wisdom on what is happening when prizes are judged tends to take three forms. The first is the one expressed above that the arts prize is essentially a "lottery in which, you hope, the better books get the most tickets" (Michael Holroyd, author and prize judge, *The Guardian*, October 9, 1996). Or as another judge put it: "[J.M.] Coetzee [1999 Booker winner] has won a lottery not a literary competition" (John Sutherland, *The Guardian*, October 6, 1999). The second version of conventional wisdom is that judges apply an enlightened rationality – they make a judgement, and their deliberations establish a short list of the best and a worthy winner.

One Whitbread judge explained his role: "I think *Harry Potter* is derivative, dull and boring. That may make me a pompous prat but so be it. That's my judgment and that was what I was being asked for" (Anthony Holden, *Daily Telegraph*, January 27, 2000). The novelist and Booker judge, Ruth Rendell, saw her task in similarly stark terms: "We were constantly asked while judging what it was we looked for and we always answered: the best book. There can be no other criterion" (*Daily Telegraph*, November 4, 1995).

The third form of conventional wisdom is that prizes are the product of some kind of corruption. In her novel *Gaveston*, Stephanie Merritt (2002: 34) imagines a media tycoon who sponsors a literary prize "that was consistently, for the three years of its existence, won by his own authors." This sort of assumption colors almost all accounts of France's Prix Goncourt for literature, where it is claimed that the same three publishers effectively dominate the process and fix the result (Goff 1989). When the model and actress Jerry Hall was selected as a Whitbread judge, the choice was defended in terms of Hall's incorruptability: "She is not part of the scene. She has not been compromised by years of friendship and rivalry, by favours given and received. She has not taught on a creative writing course. She does not need to ingratiate herself with a publisher" (Terence Blacker, *The Independent*, December 14, 1999). The implication was, of course, that most other judges were in some way corrupted.

These three forms of conventional wisdom – the rational, the random and the corrupt – sit at various stages of remove from other accounts given by those who participate in the process, and who are keen to invest the prize with a different rhetoric. Here the story is one of a passionate engagement that defies the rational, the random and the corrupt. Simon Frith, chair of the Mercury Music Prize panel, remarked: "...once you get in that [jury] room and start fighting it out, you forget everything that's gone on outside and you become wrapped in this internal world" (quoted in *The Independent*, September 15, 1994). Judging is, says Frith, "a process which ignores political influence, but is passionate, fairly crazed and based on personal choice" (*Music Week*, September 24, 1994). The judges' discussion for the 1995 Booker was described in similar terms by the participants; it was "colossally passionate" (*The Times*, November 8, 1995). In these accounts, deliberately intended to promote the integrity of the prize, judging is a product of the passion generated in a self-contained world. It is not the product of external forces or chance; nor is it simply the exercise of cool reason.

Given these competing portraits, how are we to make sense of the judging process? It is true that we can, for instance, find evidence of corruption, or at least doubtful practices – judges who are related to nominees, judges with commercial interests in nominees, and so on – but it would be hard to produce sufficient evidence to make this true of all prizes at all times. Writing about his extensive experience of judging, Michael Holroyd claimed: "I have never been bribed or bullied, never been handed a brown envelope or given a sub-poena" (*The Guardian*, October 9, 1996). Another judge reported that the Booker prize "is gloriously free from corruption" (Jason Cowley, *The Times*, October 14, 1997). While the organizers of the Whitbread were convinced that, even if bribes were offered, "outside persuasion could never sway a judge" (*The Independent*, November 19, 1989). It is, of course, true that such people would say this about the prizes with which they are involved, but my research has not revealed any evidence of systematic corruption. Equally, the claim that the results are random or a lottery is not sustained by anything more than strongly held views about what *should* have won. The fact that the result is surprising or unpredictable does not, in itself, make it random. To claim that it was would be to suggest that all such gatherings produce random results: job interviews, criminal juries, cabinets, board meetings. Why are literary judging panels to be treated as different to these other, similar forms of judging? Thus rather than start from the traditional forms of conventional wisdom, my intention is to explore judging from the assumption that it is a rationally reconstructable process engaged in by reasonable people. This means assuming that judging arts prizes is like any other such processes of decision making. To say this is, of course, not to say much. It begs important questions about how we might reconstruct the process, especially given the fact that these deliberations are necessarily kept secret. One way to explore the operations of the prize jury is to ask whether it might replicate other procedures and processes about which more is known.

ANALOGIES AND COMPARISONS

Use of terms like "judging" and "juries" suggests the obvious analogy with the criminal system. Indeed, the journalist Robert Macfarlane once proposed: "Ideally, the Booker Prize would be run like a criminal trial. Past offences (or past novels) would not be taken into account, and justice would be administered only according to the available evidence (the books in question)" (*The Observer*, November 5, 2000). So too, the novelist A.S. Byatt described her experience of judging a literary award as like sitting on a criminal jury (*Sunday Times*, October 15, 1989). There are obvious differences between the two types of jury, of course, but they both require that a group of disparate people reach agreement by a variety of methods – from advocacy to voting.

Certainly, research into the operation of trial juries provides some suggestive lines of inquiry. Using shadow juries (a panel of people who hear the same evidence as the real jury, but whose deliberations are available to researchers) has revealed that there was very little movement in opinion over the course of discussion and people tend to hold to the same view that they had when they entered the jury room for the first time (McCabe and Purves 1974). A similar conclusion was reached by other researchers who saw jury discussion as serving to "clarify and solidify initial positions" (Hans and Vidmar 1986: 112). There is some evidence that this picture accords with that of literary prize juries. One Whitbread judge remarked: "I was open to persuasion, and I was not moved to change my mind" (Simon Tait, *The Independent*, January 29, 1996). And one of the organizers of the Whitbread prize told me: "probably within the first 30 minutes, from their discussions with each other, I will know who the winner's going to be... They come into the meeting and they cut a lot of the crap immediately, to the extent that they're sending external messages to each other." As if to confirm this view that minds are made up early on, one Mercury Music Prize judge said: "If you're talking about an album and you just realize that nobody else is getting it, you might as well give up" (interview with the author). To this extent, the analogy with the law-court jury may be instructive, but it may not be the best comparison. As Ruth Rendell wrote in the diary she kept while judging the Booker Prize: "We judges – judges, surely, not jury, as common usage has it; a jury decides guilt and innocence, not merit" (*Daily Telegraph*, November 4, 1995).

A better analogy might be the academic job-selection committee, except that the incentives are more sharply focused: you have to work with the favored candidate – you don't have to read or listen to the winner, or display their work in your front room. Jeremy Treglown, who has chaired several literary prizes and job-selection panels, argued that the analogy has some validity (interview with author), but other prize judges have used a different academic comparison: the seminar or tutorial. Booker judge Helen McNeil described her first encounter with her fellow judges as a "very civilized" discussion of the nature of English literature (interview with author). In doing so, she echoed the biographer Victoria Glendenning's experience of judging sessions as having "the civil but highly charged atmosphere of a literary seminar," in much the same way that the writer Margaret Forster compared judging to taking part in a "very long tutorial" (*Sunday Times*, October 17, 1982). Taking the comparison further, one of the Booker panels actually awarded grades – from A to D – to the contending books, as if they were so many undergraduate essays (Brian Aldiss, *The Guardian*, October 9, 1981).

Crudely, the fact that these analogies work to a variable extent is suggestive of the thought that the random outcome assumption remains suspect. At the same time, it does not take us very far in making sense of the process of judging. Rather than asking what kind of institution the judging panel resembles, it is perhaps better to think of it as a process for reaching decisions. Once again, a variety of disciplinary approaches might be called forth, but for the purposes of this article, I want to use the insights and approaches of politics. Each of the following three sections explores the extent to which insights and ideas drawn from politics can help us to understand the judgements reached by prize juries.

COLLECTIVE CHOICES AND DECISION RULES

Martyn Goff, organizer of the Booker Prize, has said: "Most critics of the [Booker] prize and the choices and everything else totally underestimate the chemistry of five people. When they meet together for the first time, when they don't know each other … as they meet more and more so there are hidden antipathies, dislikes, all sorts of things, and this affects the judging" (interview with author). In the social sciences, the idea of a "personal chemistry" affecting the outcome of decisions has been translated into the psychology of "groupthink" (Janis 1972) or into paradoxes of rational choices preferences (Dunleavy 1991). The first refers to the ways in which a distinct collective perspective, one that the individuals themselves (qua individuals) do not hold; the second to the way that individually rational decisions can produce collectively irrational outcomes (and vice versa). Both ideas are captured in A.S. Byatt's comment: "I don't believe that any group chooses the 'best book' that its individual members, by and large, would have chosen, left to themselves" (*Sunday Times*, October 15, 1989). The result of deliberation is never the simple product of addition, because any aggregation itself entails implicit and explicit judgements about the appropriate method, and this in turn encodes particular values and interests.

If the judging process is seen as an exercise in collective decision making, then it follows that the methods for reaching those decisions need to be the focus of analysis. As Kenneth Shepsle and Mark Bonchek (1997: 177; their emphasis) argue: "The decisions a group reaches … depend not only on the degree to which group members reveal or misreveal their preferences, but also on the way they conduct the actual decision making. And all those other things, likewise, are influenced by the voting method we adopt. A group decision surely reflects member preferences. *But it also reflects much more.*" Applied to prize committees, therefore, this approach focuses our attention on such things as the administration of the meeting and the voting procedures. Changes in the rules, about the number of nominations on the shortlist, about who can be nominated, about how the longlist is compiled, can affect the outcome. (As one prize chair acknowledged: "instead of a couple of lunches, we [could] have a three- or four-day discussion in which every book is talked about" [interview with author].) Adopting different procedures produces different results.

How the meeting is chaired, how the agenda is set, how the vote is taken: all these have profound and decisive effects upon the outcome of any meeting. It seems unlikely that prize committees are the exception to this rule. One chair of a prize used a system of elimination, excluding those books deemed to have no chance of winning, while another introduced a point scheme, whereby each judge gave six points to their first choice, five to their second, and so on. Some prizes (e.g. the David Cohen Prize for literature) use a secret ballot; others have an open ballot. When John Sutherland served on the Booker, he discovered that "[Gerald] Kaufman [the chair of the prize and Labour politician], dirigiste to the end, had decreed that every member [of the jury] had to come to the meeting with just one nomination. That is to say, no open minds. No voting, just majority decision and no lingering" (*The Guardian*, October 6, 1999). Judges of the 1996 Booker wrote to the *Independent on Sunday* (23 March 1997) to confirm that "choosing a winner by majority vote is normal practice among Booker panels." But as rational-choice theorists and others have pointed out almost all majorities are in some sense fictional (Arrow 1951; Dahl 1956; McLean 1987). They are the artificial product of decision rules, and different rules produce a different "majority" choice. This might explain how, according to the journalist Paul Levy, "in 1994 a virtually unreadable book, James Kelman's *How Late It Was, How Late,* won as a last minute compromise in confused circumstances when the chairman, John Bayley, called for another vote after the book he favoured had won – as he did not wish to appear to have influenced unduly the voting" (*Wall Street Journal*, August 11, 1995). In a similar vein, one Booker judge reported how under pressure of the deadline for their decision and "Exasperated, we stumble on an impromptu marking system, evaluating books in the manner of ice-skaters. The first round of this farrago is inconclusive, although frontrunners are emerging. Under the eye of the clock, we vote again..." (Jason Cowley, *The Times*, October 14, 1997).

In setting up voting rules to produce results, whether under time pressures or other problems, juries create a perfect opportunity for tactical voting – supporting a candidate not because he or she is your first preference, but because it enables you to prevent your least preferred candidate from winning. The result is a majority, but not the aggregation of first preferences. In general elections, tactical voting is risky and complex because of the uncertainties in the information on which it is based (about which party has the best chance of winning; about what they each stand for). With prizes, the process is much more transparent, and it is therefore easier to see what tactics to use. With the Whitbread in 2000, "one judge said he felt he had to resort to tactical voting to ensure that anyone but [J.K. Rowling's Harry] Potter won" (*The Times*, January 27, 2000).

During the 1989 Whitbread prize discussions, two authors (Salman Rushdie and A.N. Wilson) tied with four votes each; while their rivals, Paul Sayer and Peter Porter, had two votes and one vote respectively. A second vote was taken, and two jurors switched to Sayer; following further discussion, two further defections occurred and another secret ballot was held. Sayer ended up winning, despite having started with half the support of the leading contenders (*The Guardian*, January 25, 1989; *The Times*, January 30, 1989). Such a phenomenon is familiar to those who study committee procedures and the instability of voting coalitions. Sayer won on the basis of second preferences, and on the basis of the intensity with which negative preferences were held – some judges were more determined to "stop Rushdie" than they were committed to any particular winner (*The Times*, January 30, 1989).

These characteristics of collective behavior help explain, for example, why there were only five rather than six books Booker shortlisted in 1995. As one of the judges, Kate Kellaway, noted: "though every judge could easily have found a sixth, each one would have offended at least three other judges" (*The Observer*, November 5, 1995). When Arundhati Roy won the Booker in 1997, Martyn Goff was reported as saying that her novel "had the fewest objections and the strongest plusses" (*The Guardian*, October 15, 1997). Another judge described a parallel phenomenon: "I know, for instance, that whilst true enthusiasm will never, on its own, convince co-judges that a book should be short-listed, let alone win, sheer bloody-minded opposition, 'over my dead body' always works to exclude" (A.S. Byatt, *Sunday Times*, October 15, 1989). According to one of the judges, the same sort of thing occurred in the 1999 Booker when two "authors fell to the over-my-dead-body objections of two other committee members," and the eventual winner was "admired" by everyone but "no one passionately liked" (John Sutherland, *The Guardian*, October 6, 1999). Recalling his experience of judging piano competitions, Charles Rosen (2002: 103) observed: "The jury is rarely willing to be shocked, and it will too often value simple adequacy over eccentric originality."

What is interesting about this negative push factor in voting is not only that it is used against particular artists, but that it also may work against *certain types of art*. Martin Amis (2000: 46) makes this point about his own and his father's (not altogether happy) experience of prizes: "our novels are not good at creating a consensus" (a feature that, he adds, might be deemed a virtue of them). Put another way: there are certain types of book that are easier to defend than others. They are seen to have a "nobility" or "worthiness" that disarms criticism. One Booker chair, the ex-politician George Walden, recalled how difficult it was to criticize Pat Barker's *The Ghost Road*, because it evinced, he said, a moral impeccability that was hard to attack (interview with author). Another kind of novel that benefits is the formally well-written novel – with a clear drive (stylistic or narrative) and an achieved goal. Under this logic, "consistency" becomes an important criterion. "Spiky" books were less easily defended. "Booker-type decision making works against books that can be attacked" and "well-rounded books tend to win," concluded the literary critic and judge, Helen McNeil (interview with author). As one prize organizer observed:

> One of the things I've noticed is that a slightly experimental novel ... which is doing extremely well, and then ... when a major flaw is pointed out, then another judge will say "funny you should say that, because there's that very awkward chapter"

> and steadily it builds up, … whereas the lesser novel hasn't got any obvious flaws [and] manages to get through. (Interview with author)

An intriguing case study of the judging process is provided by the Booker Prize in 1989. Notes of the meeting in the Book Trust's archive record the five judges' initial preferences, out of which the longlist is constructed. No book receiving fewer than three nominations made it to the shortlist, but one book supported by all five judges failed to make the shortlist, as did another with four nominations. Such instances might be cases of what A.S. Byatt describes as the "attractive, witty, elegant books that always make the shortlist, and then become less attractive with subsequent readings" (*Sunday Times*, October 15, 1989). Equally, they may be examples of cases in which all judges had a weak preference for a novel, but none felt absolutely committed to it. Such outcomes are not simply a "natural" product of the aggregation of preferences. They are the result of engineering: the way chairs conduct meetings, take votes, set agendas and so on.

Because of their awareness of the quirks of committee behavior, some juries and their chairs also take steps to resist the tendency toward consensus around second favorites or against experimental works. One Booker panel, for example, decided to prohibit reading aloud, because this enabled people to add a sarcastic, dismissive tone (Booker judge, interview with author). Jeremy Treglown, who has chaired both the Whitbread and the Booker, made it an article of faith "to produce a clear and interesting decision, rather than a compromise decision… Chairing does involve, I think, trying to push people in that sort of direction [i.e. going for the best, not accepting second best]" (interview with author). When George Walden chaired the Booker, he drew on his political and diplomatic experience. He wanted to prevent his committee from becoming deadlocked or irreconcilably divided. He knew from his experience as a diplomat that "just having a meeting" was hopeless: everyone just ends up disagreeing. As chair, you needed to know in advance what everyone thinks, and also what you want to happen. But Walden was not interested only in reaching decisions. He also wanted a certain *kind* of decision, one which was not tainted by compromise and "populism" ("a Roddy Doyle-type decision," as he characterized it). His practice of entertaining the judges, of allowing them to get to know each other, was inspired by the idea that they would come to trust each other, as well as learning about each other's predilections. The effect of this, claimed Walden, was to create an atmosphere where compromise – "the middle option" – was not the inevitable outcome (interview with author). In chairing the Mercury Music Prize, Simon Frith resisted the use of votes in order to get people to think about the "sense of the meeting" and not just to promote their own view (email to author).

What this section reveals is that certain aspects of jury behavior can be accounted for in terms of the decision rules implemented and the steps taken to modify their impact. The important insight implicated in this is that the choice of rules affects not only the winner, but also *the type* of winner.

POWER

Although the mechanics of collective decision making are clearly important to the process of judging arts prizes, they do not tell a complete story. Or rather, in focusing on procedures, they have little to say about the resource that those procedures manage, namely "power." The literary critic Frank Kermode once wrote of his experience in judging the first Booker with the renowned writer Dame Rebecca West: "It never seemed to occur to her that her opinion of a book might reasonably be questioned, or that anybody else's deserved more than cursory consideration... In the end, the other judges felt that they had no option but to vote unanimously for her firm but not enthusiastic choice" (*Prospect*, May 2000: 58). It may be rare for a single individual to dictate an outcome (and we cannot be certain that Kermode's interpretation is accurate), but power in some form undoubtedly affects the operation of juries. One obvious source of power is that which resides in the role of chair. One literary panel chair admits to using his power as chair to get one of Martin Amis's novels onto the shortlist in the face of considerable opposition (although his power, he wryly observed, did not extend to getting the ultimate prize for Amis). This was not just a matter of the exercise of formal authority, but also of the knowledge he acquired of his panel's preferences as a result of his liaison with them (interview with author). Whatever the form or source of power, it is not absolute, and there are many examples of chairs who have failed even to get their favored author onto the shortlist (prize organizer, interview with author).

Power does not just reside with the chair. It also exists in the distribution of rhetorical skill or cultural capital around the table. The ability to articulate a particular idea or argument can have an important impact on the outcome. The organizer of the Whitbread prize observed of the judging process that judges "quite like the chucking out method, because it's a weight off their mind, because they've been keeping it on for a reason they're not quite sure about, *as soon as someone has put that into words*, they're quite happy to get rid of it" (interview with author). What this points to is the power of rhetoric – the capacity to put something "into words" and to persuade people to agree. Judging, by this account, is an exercise in the skills and power of rhetoric. Judging is about finding reasons to select or reject, and the outcome, therefore, owes much to how these reasons are supplied.

This approach to the judging process sees it as the playing out of particular cultural power relations, and as such draws on the work of Bourdieu (1984), Frith (1996) and Smith (1988). There are two elements to this. The first is the capacity to speak – the confidence to judge; the second is the ability to command an audience – to be listened to. This second element refers to the "authority" that parties to the debate can command in arguing. One Booker judge, the novelist Bernice Rubens, complained: "They [Booker judges] don't listen to novelists" (Bainbridge et al. 1999). By contrast, a chair of the Booker, Carmen Callil, wrote of her jury: They're all writers or critics so it's easier to trust their judgement" (*Sunday Times Magazine*, October 27, 1996). Either way, it is evident that judging entails establishing a basis on which people will be heard (or ignored). Being listened to, though, is not enough; it is also a matter of what is said and how it is expressed. One Booker judge reported that the least effective judge was the least articulate, the least able to say what moved him or her or what was special (interview with author). By contrast Kate Kellaway said of her fellow Booker judge Adam Mars-Jones: "this is a man who could persuade you that a chair was a table, or a turkey a swan" (*The Observer*, November 5, 1995).

Advocacy is not just a matter of skills in putting ideas into words; it is also a matter of the authority that certain languages command. If the debate about the relative merits of a piece of music is conducted on musicological criteria, those with access to the appropriate language and terms will be at an advantage. The administrator of the Booker was quoted as saying that the Whitbread's decision to include Jerry Hall as a judge would never work because "these people [celebrities] speak a different language. When the other judges talk about form and narrative dialogue, they are left in the dark" (*The Independent*, December 14, 1999). Although the Booker has, in fact, used "celebrities" such as Mary Wilson, writer of light verse and wife of ex-Prime Minister Harold Wilson, the pressure to choose members of the literary elite has been a constant feature of the prize.[2] This chimes with those accounts of the judging process as some version of the university seminar or tutorial. Certainly, the earliest Booker panels appeared to be composed of those rich in intellectual cultural capital. In 1970, the list of possible judges included: Saul Bellow, Angus Wilson, F.R. Leavis, George Steiner, Tony Tanner, Christopher Ricks (Minutes, Booker Prize Committee, 10 September 1970).

What appears to happen is that certain languages and rhetorics are organized into the discussion and some organized out. That this occurs is partly to be explained by the fact that different cultural professions work with different critical discourses. This argument is made by Frith, both in his capacity as a Mercury judge and as a writer on esthetics (e.g. Frith 1996). The background of judges seems to him to be reflected in the way they approach the task of judging: "the way music journalists work is that they tend to operate in an exclusive fashion, in other words a lot of critics seem to focus on things that only a few people are going to like – exclusivity, whereas if you work in radio you're more interested in trying to put an audience together" (interview with author). As if to illustrate this, one Mercury judge, the musician Anne Dudley, once talked of her (vain) attempt to persuade her fellow judges to vote for the Manic Street Preachers' *Everything Must Go*: "It really did attempt to break new ground in terms of its arrangements. It was a fantastic sound – the clarity of the texture, very interesting use of strings... I couldn't really get the others to agree with me. They kept saying 'Sounds like Queen to me'. Well, what can you say? Well, *yes*, it does a *bit...*" (*The Guardian*, April 10, 1998; her emphasis). Another Mercury judge, explaining the decision to give the award to Talvin Singh, said that his "record works as a movement in the classical sense. The composers on the panel, for instance, admired it for that reason. They want to know how the overall concept is expressed and how well it sustains. They talk about note and key changes" (*The Guardian*, September 10, 1999). Yet another Mercury judge explained how, although the jury was not much impressed by one jazz record, they were impressed by the fact that the judge who was "the real jazz expert" liked it, and as a result were persuaded to put it on the shortlist; in the same way, they acknowledged that the "classical composers [on the Mercury] have a better ear for the classical stuff" (interview with author). Frith argued that the skills of the advocate are crucial to the outcome: "What matters is less comparison than advocacy. It's a pity that no one outside the judging room will ever hear the wonderful case made (by the same judge) as to why first *To Bring You My Love* and then *Maxinquaye* should win the prize; that no one else will get to applaud the speech that swung it for Portishead" (*The Guardian*, September 15, 1995).

It is one thing, however, to observe the different critical discourses and the ways in which they clash and coincide. It is another to explain why some triumph. Why, for example, do women do less well out of literary prizes? Of the twenty-nine winners of the Booker until 1996, only ten were women (Todd 1996: 83–5). Between 1985 and 1996, the Whitbread prize had nominated only two women for the novel category. Only six of the forty winners of the W.H. Smith's prize have been women. *The Independent* calculated that in the ten years to 1996, £308,000 in prize money had gone to men, and £102,000 to women (January 27, 1996). (The Orange Prize for literature by women was one response to this state of affairs.) This is compounded by the general underrepresentation of women on prize juries (Street 2002). These explicit forms of power and discrimination may be reflected in less immediately evident forms. When Helen McNeil was a Booker judge in 1989, there were no informal, get-to-know-you sessions between the judges. Quite the opposite: the first two meetings (for the longlist and shortlist) were held at the Athaneum Club. Only men were entitled to be members, and the two women judges were shepherded in by the side door. The meeting was held in the gentleman's club atmosphere of the library and its leatherbound volumes. The judging was done in an environment in which the women felt at a cultural disadvantage.[3] Another woman judge talked of feeling "alone" because she was a woman. Her views were listened to, but she was not part of the same world as the judges who knew each other already. Other women judges, asked about this, were reluctant to suggest any discrimination, although one of these who denied that gender made a difference did note that men tended to regard themselves as "keepers of the canon" (interviews with author).

In thinking about the way discourses form part of the relations of power, of this policing by stealth, we need to note that gender is just one possible dimension. In 1989, it was speculated that Whitbread's commercial interests might have influenced the decision not to award the prize (that bore its name) to Alexander Stuart's *The War Zone* (the original choice for winner) because its subject matter – incest – was not good for the corporate image. Such speculations were dismissed by other observers (*Publishers News*, November 17, 1989). Others refer to the "insidious tyranny" of literary fashion on jury decisions; these derive from the politics of the publishing industry, rather than the interests of sponsors. The disillusioned Booker judge Nicholas Mosley wrote of his experience: "It was as if my fellow judges were following a fashionable literary trend which held that the idea that a novel might contain any 'message', that a writer should have anything to 'say', was indeed an illusion: a novel was simply a text from which it was the job of the readers to extract what they liked" (*Sunday Times*, October 16, 1994). There was no place for novels that were "good reads."

Some of these claims can be subsumed within the general thought that the prizes are created to reward certain kinds of achievement rather than others. The Booker's format guarantees that it eliminates genre fiction, and hence the underrepresentation of popular writers (like Iain Banks or Ian Rankin). The organizer of the Orange Prize, Kate Mosse, saw the hegemony of the Booker as working to impose "a very narrow definition of what Literature with a capital L actually is. It therefore excludes all genre writing, even though many genre books transcend limits" (quoted in *The Guardian*, March 25, 1996). In other words, the way critical authority was legitimated or marginalized was important to the outcome.

The suggestion here, in this discussion of power in the judging process, is that any analysis of prize decisions must be sensitive to the ways in which critical judgement is established and legitimated (or undermined). The operation of juries serves to silence some voices and to give authority to others. In this sense, the prize jury is a microcosm of wider processes that organize esthetic evaluation (e.g. Bourdieu 1984; Smith 1988; Frith 1996), and of the ways in which rhetoric is used to give force to ideas and arguments (e.g. Chilton and Schaffner 2002; Fairclough 2003). These are directly analogous to political processes of rhetoric and persuasion (Jorgenson et al.

1998; Koch 1998). The judging of prizes entails the playing out of discourses of power, organized through representations of authority as well as through the pragmatics of committee management. And in this process, power operates to privilege certain cultural forms and expressions, to give legitimacy to some types of artistic expression and some types of critical language and criteria.

DEMOCRACY AND DELIBERATION

If arts prize juries follow the rules of political reality, they also aspire to a political ideal. They represent themselves as democracies. They see themselves as embodying (different) forms of democratic deliberation and democratic procedure. Thus one judge records: "I'd grown incredibly attached to my two personal favourites...Nevertheless, democracy rules and ... I reluctantly went with the otherwise unanimous vote" (Mariella Frostrup, *The Observer*, November 12, 2000). Others place emphasis on the deliberative character of their discussions. One of the Mercury Music Prize judges explained how Gomez's *Bring It On* became the eventual winner: "It seemed such a frail contender when it first found its way on to the shortlist of 12 albums and was initially derided in some quarters as unauthentic, retro blues-rock. But over time *Bring It On* gradually revealed a wealth of detail in the production" (David Sinclair, Mercury judge, *The Times*, September 18, 1998). While these quotations from judges reveal only their perceptions or rationalizations of the process, what they do indicate is the general tendency to legitimate the prize in terms of its democratic character.

What they aspire to is a view of the deliberative process as transforming private, partial preferences into a collective view on the best choice (Fishkin 1996). What counts as the "best" is not a simple majority, but rather a collective view, first, on what counts as "the best," and, second, what meets those criteria. Or as David Miller (1992: 62) explains, the deliberative process transforms "initial policy preferences (which may be based on private interest, sectional interest, prejudice and so on) into ethical judgements on the matter in hand." Miller is writing about political judgement in a democracy, but a similar logic may apply to judging prizes, to the extent that, whatever the interests gathered round the table, these are modified, and even transformed, by the dialog.

The suggestion here is that in understanding judging processes it is important to be aware too of the democratic ideals that inform and legitimate the business. There is a belief that judges are acting as equals and for some common good, and that such processes may be defensible in just these terms. To this extent, therefore, we might reasonably analyze prize judging as a form of democracy. But what they are also doing, and this may be even more important, is setting the criteria by which "quality" or "value" are assigned. Juries are not simply processing a decision via preestablished criteria or procedures. They are also creating those criteria and procedures in terms of some notion of "the good."

CONCLUSION

As we noted at the beginning, there are those who argue that prize juries are selecting the best, and that this is an objective exercise – a task that entails simply applying critical insight. This assumption is implicated in accusation that such and such a panel got it wrong, or in this comment from the Literary Editor of *The Observer*: "So. Of course *Beowulf* [a version by Seamus Heaney] should have been made the Whitbread Book of the Year. What is truly incredible, among the many incredible, even farcical, things that have emerged about the judging of this year's prize is that nine very intelligent, educated people should have had any trouble at all in deciding between a critically-acclaimed version of a 3,000 line Old English masterpiece and a popularly venerated contemporary fairytale for articulate 10–year-olds [*Harry Potter and the Prisoner of Azkaban*]" (*The Observer*, January 30, 2000). The evidence discussed here suggests that such a perception of prize juries and their practices misses much of what is going on. Without pretending to provide a definitive portrait, this article has pointed to the political processes embedded in the jury's behavior. These processes are to be found in the choice and effects of the decision rules, the distribution and character of power, and the political ideals to which they aspire. These practices help to constitute the judging process and to shape its (intended and unintended) results.

The processes and their impact are revealing of the ways in which esthetic judgement is constructed, and by implication this article suggests ways in which those judgements might themselves be judged or changed. For although they clearly do not represent the imposition of established standards, equally they are not random. And while it may make little sense to say that it was "wrong" or "right" for a prize to be awarded to X or Y, we are in a position to comment on the ways in which X or Y was judged. We can in this sense argue for other, politically preferable, more democratic methods for reaching these conclusions. As Rosen (2002: 106) notes of one piano competition he was involved in: "The reason for the lamentable misjudgement was a flawed voting system used that year."

This focus on the political dimensions of the operation of the arts prize jury has made eclectic use of political science methods and insights. In doing so, I have not tried or intended to produce a single model, and indeed there are tensions and contradictions between the approaches used. My justification for this is that this is a work of exploration. It is not intended to capture a definitive picture, but rather to see how esthetic judgement can be read and understood politically. It does not rule out other approaches. The point is to understand arts prizes better and the implications they have for our understanding of the way in which esthetic judgement operates as political practice.

As we noted earlier, prizes matter. They not only reward artists directly, but they also generate further sales, which, in turn, increase the artist's commercial bargaining power. Prizes impact too on the operation of cultural industries and institutions, affecting commissioning and subsidizing decisions. What this study of the arts prize has revealed is that the awarding of the prize (which then generates these various effects) can be understood as a political process that may, in some cases, produce a particular kind of art, art that tends to the "well-formed" rather than the experimental. The arts prize, in this sense, links political values and practices to esthetic judgements.

NOTES

The research reported here was funded by the Nuffield Foundation. My thanks is due to all those interviewed for the project, and to the Book Trust for access to their archives. For comments on earlier versions of this article, I also owe thanks to Simon Frith, John Armitage and the anonymous referees of this journal.

1. As with many other such decision making bodies, arts juries are necessarily secretive bodies and reluctant to discuss in detail their deliberations (or to grant direct access to them). This research addresses this problem by using as many different sources as possible, including media reports, formal archives and personal interviews.
2. Terence Kilmartin, Literary Editor of the *Observer*, wrote to the organisers of the Booker in 1970, when the prize was a year old, to voice his disapproval of judges selected on the grounds of "personality" or their associations with the "book trade." The ability to judge literary merit should be the only criterion. (Letter to the Publishers Association, 16 May 1970)
3. Ten years later, Mariella Frostrup referred to the final judging taking place in "an intimidating mayoral room in London's Guildhall" (*The Observer*, November 12, 2000).

REFERENCES

Amis, M. 2000. *Experience*. London: Jonathan Cape.

Arrow, K.J. 1951. *Social Choice and Individual Values*. New York: Wiley.

Bainbridge, B., Cowley, J., Goff, M. and Rubens, B. 1999. "Open Booker." London: Royal Overseas League. 20 October.

Bourdieu, P. 1984. *Distinction: A Social Critique of the Judgement of Taste*. London: Routledge.

Burn, G. 1987. "Title Fight." *Arena*, Autumn, pp. 36–41.

Caves, R. 2000. *Creative Industries: Contracts Between Art and Commerce*. Cambridge: Harvard University Press.

Chilton, P. and Schaffner, C. (eds). 2002. *Politics as Text and Talk*. Amsterdam: John Benjamins Publishing.

Dahl, R. 1956. *A Preface to Democratic Theory*. Chicago: Chicago University Press.

Dunleavy, P. 1991. *Democracy, Bureaucracy and Public Choice*. Hemel Hempstead: Harvester Wheatsheaf.

Fairclough, N. 2003. *Analysing Discourse: Textual Analysis for Social Research*. London: Routledge.

Fishkin, J. 1996. "Bringing Deliberation to Democracy: The British Experiment." *The Good Society*, 5(3): 45–9.

Frith, S. 1996. *Performing Rites: On the Value of Popular Music*. Oxford: Oxford University Press.

Goff, M. (ed.). 1989. *Prize Writing*. London: Hodder and Stoughton.

Hans, V. and Vidmar, N. 1986. *Judging the Jury*. New York: Plenum.

Janis, I. 1972. *Victims of Groupthink*. Boston: Houghton-Mifflin.

Jorgensen, C., Kock, C. and Rorbech, L. 1998. "Rhetoric That Shifts Votes: An Exploratory Study of Persuasion in Issue-oriented Public Debates." *Political Communication*, 15(3): 283–99.

Koch, J.W. 1998. "Political Rhetoric and Political Persuasion." *Public Opinion Quarterly*, 62(2): 209–29.

McCabe, S. and Purves, R. 1974. *The Shadow Jury at Work*. Oxford: Blackwell.

McLean, I. 1987. *Public Choice: An Introduction*. Oxford: Blackwell.

Merritt, S. 2002. *Gaveston*. London: Faber & Faber.

Miller, D. 1992. "Deliberative Democracy." *Political Studies*, XL, Special Issue on Democracy: 54–67.

Rosen, C. 2002. *Piano Notes: The Hidden World of the Pianist*. London: Allen Lane.

Shepsle, K. and Bonchek, M. 1997. *Analyzing Politics: Rationality, Behavior and Institutions*. New York: W.W. Norton.

Smith, B.H. 1988. *Contingencies of Value*. Cambridge: Harvard University Press.

Street, J. 2002. "The Arts Prize: Organising Popular Taste and Influencing Cultural Policy." In S. Janssen et al. (eds), *Trends and Strategies in the Arts and Cultural Industries*. Rotterdam: Barjjesteth van Waalwijk van Doorns & Co., pp. 241–54.

Todd, R. 1996. *Consuming Fictions: The Booker Prize and Fiction in Britain Today*. London: Bloomsbury.

CULTURAL POLITICS   VOLUME 1, ISSUE 2
PP 233–242

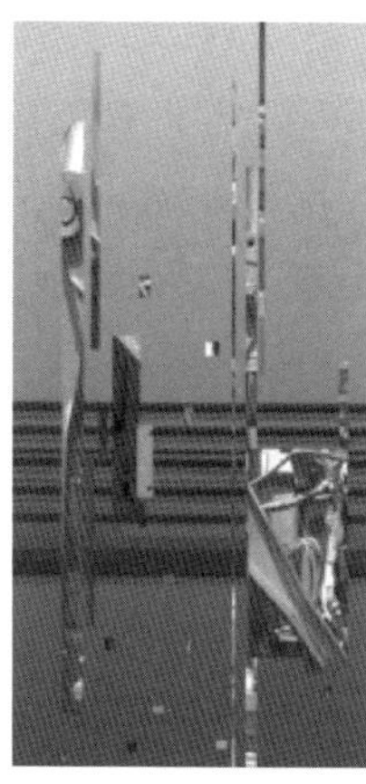

FIELD REPORT

BREAKING THE SURFACE

JOANNA GRIFFIN

JOANNA GRIFFIN IS AN ARTIST FROM THE UK WHERE SHE HAS HELD LECTURING POSTS IN FINE ART AT THE UNIVERSITY OF SOUTHAMPTON AND THE UNIVERSITY OF WOLVERHAMPTON. HER FILMS, VIDEO INSTALLATIONS, BOOK WORKS AND PRINTS HAVE BEEN EXHIBITED IN GALLERY SPACES, EVENTS AND SCREENINGS INTERNATIONALLY. CURRENTLY WORKING OUTSIDE THE UK, SHE IS PRESENTING AND DEVELOPING PROJECTS RELATING TO THE INVISIBLE ARCHITECTURE OF ORBITING SATELLITES.

ABSTRACT   Research for an arts project is often as much about the experience of looking for information as the findings themselves. This article is about an investigation into the presence of submarines in British waters. The research was for a new body of work that resulted in the presentation of film, installation and interactive work at festivals, in galleries and online. In this case the fieldwork, into the inevitably political realm of nuclear submarines, led to a series of uneasy situations.

> There are two locations in the British Isles where submarines harbor: the Devonport Naval Base in Plymouth, in the southwest of England, and the Clyde Naval Base at Faslane in Scotland. From these two places I watched submarines make their dignified way around Plymouth Sound or up the Firth of Clyde and likewise watched

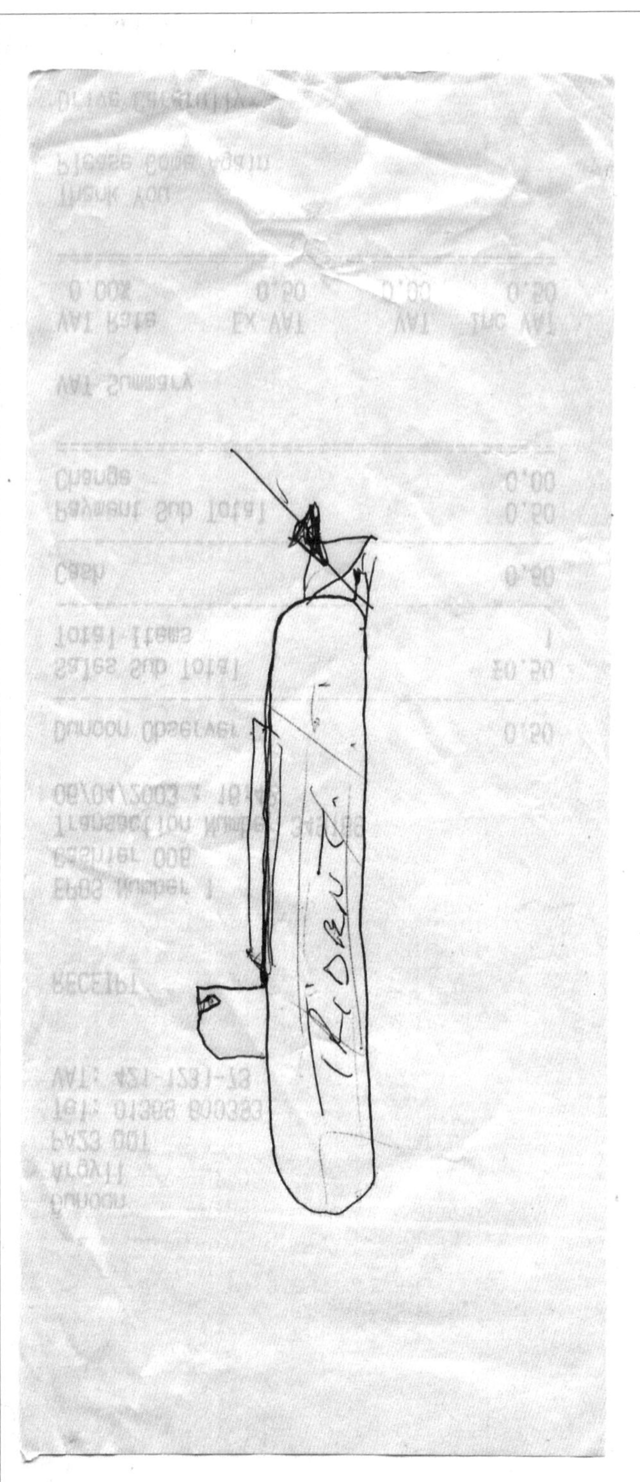

their passage out. Somewhere, away from sight of land or other boats, they submerged; their whereabouts from then on known to very few. The families of submariners only find out when the men will return by reading the daily shipping movements in the local newspaper.

This is how I tracked them; my days for a period of six months were structured by the arrivals and departures of submarines, details of which were posted in the *Western Morning News*. At first I was simply curious to see what a submarine looked like – whether they had that intangible eeriness in real life that I had seen in films. From the shore, with my video camera and tripod, I filmed submarines coming and going from Plymouth Sound and I waited too, early in the morning and after dark, for submarines that for one reason or another didn't appear at the times announced.

My investigation into the presence of submarines in the British Isles began as a foray into technomythology. I wanted to conjure the sea beast from the submarine, the damselfly from the helicopter. I once had a Sea King helicopter fly very low over me while I was walking alone in the English countryside. It turned out that the helicopter was preparing to land in a village school playground, as a treat for the last day of the school term, but as it flew over my head, huge and loud, it was a sublime experience, frightening but safe and without explanation. As an artist it made me rethink my practice. I began to work with the moving image as a way of translating compelling experience and exploring the creature-like presence that seemed to inhabit this colossal machine. With a video camera you can slow down the time you capture and reduce what you see to a small box in which these hitherto subdued references are revealed. Were they a subconscious creation of the engineers, these cartoon-like resemblances to creatures, a by-product of an overambitious determination to make rational killing machines, or did the designers deliberately draw on B-movie horror and science fiction to elicit irrational fear?

The submarine's mixture of associations: its creature-like design, based originally on the sperm whale, its role in covert military operations together with its much-caricatured periscope render it both terrifying and ridiculous. Central to its success as a weapon is the submarine's invisibility. The tiles that clad submarines make them resistant to sonar detection and so invisible that during the Cold War, Russian and American submarines accidentally nudged each other under the polar ice. Its draw for submariners is difficult to understand. As a "boy's toy" the submarine lacks the speed and

maneuverability of an airplane and there can be few craft for which the experience of the interior and exterior can be so different. The cramped and airless living quarters give no sense of being within the sea. Yet it has always been a fearful weapon with power extending beyond its technical capabilities; the black silhouette of a conning tower breaking the surface taps into a deep mythology of sea beasts and a primordial recognition of danger.

The time I have spent hunting submarines and tracking helicopters has been a quest to come closer to this strange mythology of associations within modern hard-edged technology. But it has been a nervous exploration. Being drawn to something as deeply offensive, immoral and dangerous as the dark curves of a Hunter-Killer submarine is uncomfortable. I kept going because the ambivalence of attraction and repulsion is fascinating and difficult to define. It is a kind of hovering between states of perception, at a cusp, where on one side you understand the despicableness of war machines and on the other the same machine lets you glimpse an imagined world where whale-like creatures come close into shore. It also intrigued me that I was investigating for sites of submarine activity in the Scottish lochs where the mythology of the sea beast is such a potent and discussed element of the landscape.

In the British Library I came across a book entitled *An Essay on the Credibility of the Existence of the Kraken, Sea Serpent and other Sea Monsters* published in 1849. It attempted to give reasoned explanations for enigmatic observations at sea such as the following:

Upon the 22nd June, in lat. 46° 57' N., long. 58° 39' W., Captain Neill, of the ship "Robertson" of Greenock, then homeward bound from Montreal to Greenock, saw the head and snout of a great sea monster, of which a sketch was drawn at the time. It was first observed at about a quarter past nine A.M., on the weather-bow, about four points, and it then appeared like a large vessel lying on her beam-ends. The "Robertson" was hauled up so as to near it, and running at the rate of eight knots an hour, she, at noon, got abreast of it, distant about a mile to leeward. On observation at this time, it was discovered to be the head and snout of a great fish swimming to windward; and though an attempt was made to get closer, it could not be accomplished, because the fish, without much apparent exertion, kept swimming as fast as the vessel sailed. Immediately above the water its eye was seen like a large deephole. That part of the head which was above the water, measured about twelve feet, and its breadth or width twenty-five feet. The snout or trunk was about fifty feet long, and the sea occasionally rippled over one part, leaving other parts quite dry and uncovered. The colour of the part seen was green, with a light and dark shade, and the skin was ribbed. (Anon. 1849: 30)

Descriptions of sightings are inevitably compelling before a rationale is imposed that exposes the flaw or fake. They are detailed linear accounts describing something seen but not understood; potentially extraordinary until proven to be banal. For me the ambivalence holds a similar, hovering fascination, through partial knowledge and projection, to that elicited by the submarine. The glimpse of some suppressed, atavistic animal within a modern construction is part of the unsettling eeriness of submarines, and the inability to conceptualize this recognition is perhaps the basis of the terror they invoke.

At the beginning of the second attack on Iraq I went to Scotland to visit lochs used as submarine test sites. It was my second visit for this investigation. I began at the Loch Striven site. It was the presumed location of a film I had seen while researching in the Imperial War Museum film archive. The words "human torpedo" had come up in the index, so naturally I was curious. A human torpedo or "chariot" was a torpedo with a kind of cockpit attached, which operated like a motorized tandem by two men in frog suits. The silent film is all smiles and laughter at the self-conscious filming process, with occasional serious attention to the new procedure being revealed for the first time to a group of reporters. I found the articles in the Colindale newspaper library, dated April 19, 1944:

Like a submarine it can navigate either on the surface at "periscope depth", the periscope in this case being the commander's head, or completely below the surface. Driven by an electric motor, it is completely silent, and it is designed for use at night, so that it is practically invisible as long as it moves slowly. (*The Times* 1944a: 4)

It struck me that the two men's black, helmeted heads making way just above and below the surface of the water, causing a small v-shaped wake, were a dead ringer for the Loch Ness Monster. There had to be a connection between these secret trials of bizarre inventions and the history of inexplicable sightings in the area. One take of the disjointed footage caught the two men demonstrating the torpedo out of the water chatting and laughing on the deck. Handsome in thick Aran sweaters, the older one smoking a pipe, they joked with each other and it seemed to me that this was behavior from a past generation, from an era of inspiring bravado and courage. They would have gone through terrible hardships in developing the technology: ear injuries sustained when the torpedoes hit fresh water and plummeted hundreds of feet, the coldness making their hands virtually immovable. However, here on film was the denial of uncomfortable truths British people became so famous for. Even the newspapers reported, "The woollen clothing maintains the normal circulation of the blood, and the hands remain warm even under water" (*The Times* 1944b: 2).

At Loch Striven I hoped to find something that would make a connection to the laughing men in the film and this time of strange underwater invention. At the opening of the loch, a grey, box-shaped pontoon floated in the middle of the water. A little further down was an equally inexplicable pier consisting of theatrical arrays of pipes. Opposite this were low wooden buildings, fenced off, and a sign "Scottish NATO Pol Depots Loch Striven Installation." The road soon stopped near a small wooden jetty with its own sign "Authorised Personnel ONLY." The typeface was slightly italic and could have dated to the 1940s, the time of the film. I walked along the water for a while, but found nothing else. On the way back I stopped at the installation. I wanted to know what this strange pier of pipes was, but I took a photo of the human torpedo men so that I could seem to be asking about that. A man in uniform came up to the fence. I asked if he thought the picture was from this loch. It could have been any loch, he said, and he could not tell me what the pier of pipes was for and there was a sign that said I could not take photos, in case I hadn't seen. Usually things go better than this. I felt he was suspicious of me; I thought he might even send a report on me to someone.

Around from Loch Striven is Holy Loch. In 1961 Harold Macmillan allowed President Eisenhower to set up a base here so that American

Polaris submarines could be within striking distance of the Soviet Union. Macmillan was reluctant to agree because the densely populated city of Glasgow was close by and he knew it would lose him votes, but it was the only way Britain could afford a Polaris of its own. Holy Loch is a short loch. The submarines, up to nine of them, must have filled it, together with the depot boat on which many of the American servicemen and their families lived. I looked for artifacts again. There was very little here – grey houses, industrial units for rent, all but a ghost town. I stopped at a shop and asked the man behind the counter where the base had been. He said when the base closed in 1992 most of the personnel left with the "mother boat" and the buildings associated with the base were flattened. He said he used to work there. I felt he didn't like my amazement at this – that a man working in a shop had been a part of this infamous site but it was hard to backtrack. He said I'd struck gold with him, that most people wouldn't have known about the base and he drew me a picture of Polaris, "Poseidon" the Americans called it, with arrows pointing to the torpedo holes. He said he was still under the Official Secrets Act and that I should be careful asking questions round here; I could be picked up by plain clothes police or something.

I walked back to the car definitely worried by this. My purpose with this trip was to visit as a normal member of the public, to find out things I should be entitled to know about my country. A year before I had made my first visit to the area to go to the Faslane Naval Base. This base, just across from Holy Loch, had become the British submarine dock and after the demise of the American base it became the focus of the peace protest. Before the visit I had explained in a letter of introduction that I was an artist with a funded project and was after close-up shots of submarines. As a result, I was allowed into the base, which was protected by a fence of razor barbed wire, seven bales deep. A police launch then sped me around departing submarines so that I could get the shots I needed for my film. It was 2001, the "Centenary of the Submarine," according to the navy, and, in honor of this, eleven countries had sent submarines to Faslane for a celebration. The ones I filmed were German midget submarines, with peculiar bulbous noses and lights on the conning towers like eyes. They made extraordinary images. The ballast tanks drained out lines of white water as the bows lifted looking like prehistoric teeth. Everyone was happy to be out on the boat, and pleased I suppose to have the interest of an artist. They were philosophical about the

Peace Camp and accepted the fact that the two opposing ideologies inevitably coexist, unhappy in a way that they needed to be part of the navy operation in order to live in such stunning surroundings. I felt too ashamed and exhausted to visit the Peace Camp afterward. Too confused at what my agenda was in this project and how easy it was for me to talk to both sides with sympathy.

I had been on board a Hunter-Killer submarine in Devonport Naval Base at Plymouth, by means of the same ploy. They said I could contact some of the Navy press, they were having such bad publicity with the nuclear reactor problem disabling the T-class submarine fleet that they could do with someone saying submarines were wonderful. I sat in the officers' quarters with the commander of HMS *Talent* and I asked why there were still nuclear submarines after the Cold War. It was an uncomfortable moment. The British Navy was the best in the world. He asked me about my project, what did I want to do? It was a cross-examination. I would have said I was interested in the creature-like resemblances of submarines, but my real agenda had actually become deeply unclear to myself. I had just crouched in the emergency escape hatch with my tour guide and we had looked at the labeled cupboards. The one I remember was "barley sugar." He talked about the procedure that would be adopted in there, the chain of command, the need to occupy the men constantly. Then he stopped and looked down and for an imperceptible moment I could see it had struck him again this terrible possibility of being trapped. I could not criticize these people, under command, so hospitable to me, I had become too close.

At Holy Loch something equally unbearable sank in. That it was wrong to question the military's appropriation of the landscape, even that it was wrong to look. As I walked back to the car holding my till receipt with the drawing of a Trident submarine on it, I felt real dread at the enormity of the military operation and this invisible barrier to knowledge that I was beginning to mark out. Dread too at the normalizing of their procedures with uniforms, signage and gates while the peace protesters looked like the outlaws, the camp squeezed onto a small contested strip of land at the side of the road, just before the heavy barbed wire fences of the base began.

The next day I went to the Peace Camp. Soon after I arrived a police car drew up; apparently that was usual when someone new arrived. They wanted us to know they knew. I heard about the protests. People blockading the road, swimming across the loch and painting

the submarines. Then they took me to some of the key sites. On the other side of the loch from the base, four of us peered through the trees, two with binoculars and two with video cameras, "monitoring" the base. Then we drove round to Coulport. This is where the weapons are kept in caves. Some indescribable statistic, my guides told me, enough bombs to destroy the world three times. I came up to a junction, noted a "keep out" sign, but nevertheless kept driving up a road in the trees to a large closed gate. I turned the car round and we carried on back toward the camp. In no time, a Range Rover police car was in front of us and then, a minute later, in the mirror, another police car behind. I wasn't sure anyone else had noticed. Were we being escorted? Were there cameras in the trees? They stayed for a while and then turned off and again I was left with the same sense that there were boundaries here that I was being made to feel I had transgressed, while nearby the unarticulated means for inflicting genocide on the whole world were being given the respectability of uniformed protection.

On the way back to the bed-and-breakfast I stopped at Glen Douglas on Loch Long. The ship *Ark Royal* had been here a few weeks before, arming itself for operations in the Gulf. On breakfast television the next day I caught some of the live footage of troops entering Saddam Hussein's palace. The media spectacle located the war very far from here – this war about the illicit possession of nuclear arms.

In June 1999 three women in a leaky motorboat boarded a pontoon in Loch Goil called *Maytime*. It was full of computer equipment used in the process of "degaussing," the technology that renders submarines near-invisible to sonar detection. The women cut wires, threw what equipment could be moved overboard and then had a picnic while they waited to be arrested. The aim, of what became known as the "Maytime action," was to disable the Trident submarine program. The women were found not guilty on the grounds that they had been trying to prevent an even-greater crime. For a while it seemed the women's actions had forced a British court to uphold International Law and declare Britain's possession of nuclear arms to be illegal. Twelve months later, however, Sheriff Gimblett's ruling at Greenock Crown Court was challenged in a rare use of judicial power by the Lord Advocate in Scotland. As Britain had no plans to use its arms, the harboring of nuclear weapons was not a threat, and therefore not necessarily illegal. So the status quo was maintained.

In Britain, it is usual for the image of conflict to come from afar. The unremarkable image of a submarine slowly crossing the wake of a sailboat by a seaside town is the image of war that goes unnoticed, embedded in the landscape. It was not until I went to Ireland a few months later where there was barely a plane in the sky that I realized how steeped in military architecture the British landscape is. Before I left, I walked through pine forests in mid-Wales and three times during the morning fighter jets came through the valley. They were only visible for a few seconds and the experience was strangely exciting. Yet these constant reminders of a military presence in the landscape seep into the psychology of the British people. Centuries of militarization of the landscape lead people to accept this as normal or inevitable. The presence is quiet and undefined; there does not seem to be anything there that demands a protest. Almost imperceptibly, the military becomes part of the everyday. Complicity in foreign warfare is absorbed into the surface appearance of things.

ACKNOWLEDGMENT

The research for this investigation was funded by an Arts and Humanities Research Board Small Award 2002–2003, a University of Wolverhampton Sabbatical Award 2000–2001 and a West Midlands Arts Creative Ambition Award 2000.

REFERENCES

Anon. 1849. *An Essay on the Credibility of the Existence of the Kraken, Sea Serpents and other Sea Monsters*. London: William Tegg & Co.

The Times. 1944a. "Two men astride in Diving Suits." April 19: 4.

—— 1944b. "Hazardous Task of Two Men." May 15: 2.

CULTURAL POLITICS   VOLUME 1, ISSUE 2   REPRINTS AVAILABLE   PHOTOCOPYING   © BERG 2005
PP 243–246   DIRECTLY FROM THE   PERMITTED BY LICENSE   PRINTED IN THE UK
PUBLISHERS.   ONLY

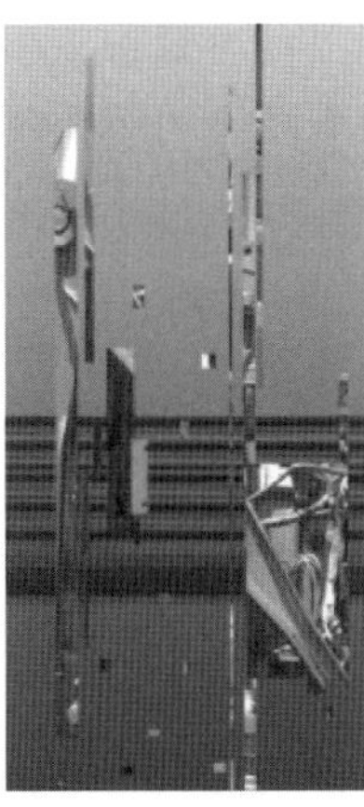

THE ALLURES AND DECEPTIONS OF DEMOCRACY

RYAN BISHOP

Inventing a Nation: Washington, Adams, Jefferson, by Gore Vidal, New Haven: Yale University Press, 2003, 208 pages, $22/£18.95 HB 0–300–10171–6

RYAN BISHOP TEACHES AT THE NATIONAL UNIVERSITY OF SINGAPORE. HE HAS PUBLISHED ON CRITICAL THEORY, MILITARY TECHNOLOGY, URBANISM AND INTERNATIONAL SEX TOURISM.

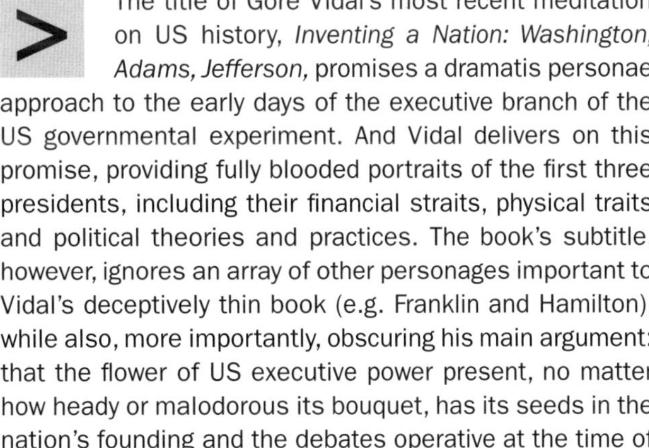

The title of Gore Vidal's most recent meditation on US history, *Inventing a Nation: Washington, Adams, Jefferson,* promises a dramatis personae approach to the early days of the executive branch of the US governmental experiment. And Vidal delivers on this promise, providing fully blooded portraits of the first three presidents, including their financial straits, physical traits and political theories and practices. The book's subtitle, however, ignores an array of other personages important to Vidal's deceptively thin book (e.g. Franklin and Hamilton), while also, more importantly, obscuring his main argument: that the flower of US executive power present, no matter how heady or malodorous its bouquet, has its seeds in the nation's founding and the debates operative at the time of its invention. The warped mirror of historical analogy and antecedent creates the funhouse of Vidal's political analyses, and it is with gleeful acumen and glib erudition that he wanders the halls of human folly known as political history, fully entranced by his subject matter and its capacity for retaining currency.

In this final installment of his trilogy on US policy, Vidal wishes to remind the citizens of "the United States of Amnesia" of several important inheritances at play in the current moment: the import of class in the founding and perpetuation of the nation; the role of property and privilege in US governance; the illusion of democracy the populace clings to; the role of the Electoral College in both thwarting majority rule and maintaining class privilege in governance; the import of capital (and debts) that funded the nation's invention; and the protection of the ruling elite from potential loss of privilege as well as protection from the tyranny of the majority through the same Constitutional mechanism of indirect representation. In other words, Vidal argues why the "election" of George Walker Bush in 2000, or rather the (re)appointment of class dominance over the popular electorate by the Supreme Court, can be traced to the nascent nation's earliest moments.

The 2000 election provides an important impetus for Vidal's historical analysis of executive power *contra* legislative tempering of said power prior to and then during the first three US administrations. The election supplies the context of Vidal's extended trope of historical analogy and antecedent, especially with regard to the roles property and privilege played then (the late eighteenth century) and now (twentieth and twenty-first centuries) within the US political system. The 2000 election pitted two American mandarins (including one distantly related to Vidal himself) against each other after the first and only US president in the twentieth century, Bill Clinton, truly up from poverty. The election and its fraught finale with the Supreme Court upholding the federal power of the Electoral College as opposed to the popular vote proved tempting for Vidal's general reading of US polity and policy. Himself a member of the American landed, privileged class, Vidal knows of what and whom he speaks.

Of significance in Vidal's analysis is the incorrect assumption operative within the US popular imagination that the nation is a democracy when it is, in fact, a three-pronged Republic designed to check both mob rule (e.g. democracy) and autocracy. Of the proposed government and its future, Franklin proved prescient in his suspicion of self-rule hogtied by indirect representation. He stated publicly at the 1787 Constitutional Convention that the government they had outlined "is likely to be well administered for a Course of Years and can only end in Despotism as other Forms have done before it, when the People shall become so corrupted as to need Despotic Government, being incapable of any other" (qtd in Vidal, pp. 30–1). Thus Vidal claims "Franklin's blunt dark prophecy" predicts "Enron ... November 2000, and following that, despotism whose traditional activity, war, now hedges us all around" (p. 31). The Electoral College has seen to the consolidation of power in the executive branch in a form one could easily construe as despotic. The cultural ethos that Vidal evokes is one shot through by the political ethos, and one he argues was foreseeable at the nation's founding. The corrupt populace of which Franklin speaks has, Vidal indirectly states, arrived.

Vidal apparently wonders about the willingness of the US population to continually swallow the duplicity, especially when it has had adequate warning from its own worried, enlightened, greedy, engaged and historically abused founders. The quotidian milieu of cultural life today reflects the corruption of political life. In this manner, and perhaps only in this manner, the US government is representative of its people. The historical evidence, though, should belie self-delusion. To make this point, Vidal parades pearls of necromantic wisdom from Washington to Adams to Franklin to Jefferson, not to mention foreign diplomats residing in the US at its founding. Consider, for example, this 1792 gem from the French minister, Fauchet: "What will be the old age of this government, if it is thus early decrepit! Such, Citizen, is the evident consequence of the system of finances devised by Mr. Hamilton. He has made a whole nation of stock-jobbing, speculating, selfish people. Riches alone fix consideration" (qtd in Vidal, p. 120). Echoes of Enron and Haliburton are meant to play in readers' ears, and they do. Consider Jefferson writing to Madison after the passage of the 1798 Sedition Act in veiled language for fear of being hauled up on sedition charges himself, "I know not what mortifies me more, that I should fear to write what I think, or my country bear such a state of things" (p. 161). The fear of postal surveillance and thought-policing conjures up the First Amendment right to free speech as being best enacted when not enacted at all that has often marked "patriotic" public discourse in US history but most recently under the Ashcroft-crafted "Patriot Act" and the general milieu of post-September 11th America.

And, consider Washington himself, global hero and first US celebrity, in his farewell address to the nation after his second term in office had ended and on the eve of the first nonmonarchical peaceful transfer of executive power:

> That nation which indulges towards another an habitual hatred or an habitual fondness, is to some degree a slave... It is a slave to its animosity, or to its affection – either of which is sufficient to lead it astray from its duty and interest. The nation urged by resentment and rage, sometimes compels the government to war, contrary to its own calculations of policy. The government sometimes participates in this propensity and dons through passion what reason would forbid it at other times; it makes the animosity of the nation subservient to hostile projects which originate in ambition and other sinister motives" (p. 126).

Ringing in these words are the antecedents of the Bush administration in its obsessive anger toward Iraq and the Blair government in its habitual fondness of the US. Thus, Vidal has George Washington warn George W. not to play king, just as he refused actual kingship. Vidal asserts that Washington's words are "applicable to our Union today as the great combine of military, media, religious mania, and lust for oil" that has "overthrown the safeguards that the first three presidents, for all their disagreements, were as one in wishing to preserve, protect, and defend" (p. 127) Washington's farewell address offers us an insight into the nature of national vilification that can lead to avoidable, unwise wars, but the warped mirror of historical analogy is rarely gazed into by those in power.

CULTURAL POLITICS   VOLUME 1, ISSUE 2
PP 247–250

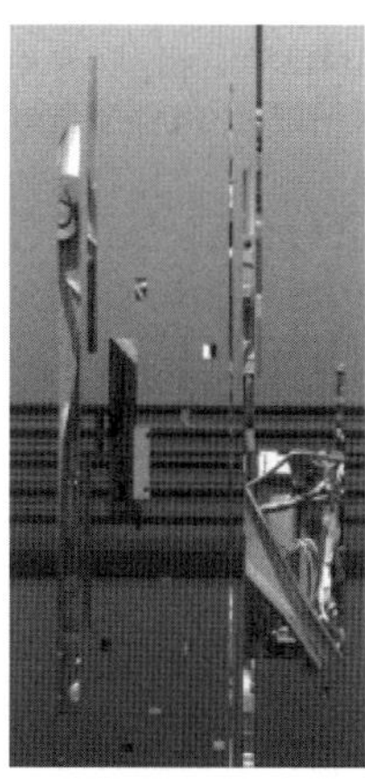

BOOK REVIEW

GOOD INTENTIONS

ALAN SINFIELD

The Globalization of Sexuality, by Jon Binnie, London: Sage, 2004, $89.95/£60, HB 0-7619-5935-1

ALAN SINFIELD WORKS ON THE SEXUAL DISSIDENCE AND CULTURAL CHANGE PROGRAM AT THE UNIVERSITY OF SUSSEX. HIS LATEST BOOK IS *ON SEXUALITY AND POWER* (COLUMBIA UNIVERSITY PRESS, 2004).

 Jon Binnie, who surely knows as much about these topics as anyone, assesses briskly the range of scholarship that has accumulated around sexuality, globalization and the local. Principal topics are the relations between the state and queerness, economic and social structures, diaspora, AIDS, postcolonial theory, migration, sex tourism and the city. Of course, these topics overlap, and in practice Binnie does not avoid repetition and redundancy (both locally, in the paragraph, and globally, across the book). *The Globalization of Sexuality* draws upon a great many published sources, affording a valuable starting point for various kinds of further work.

The founding question, in Binnie's book, is still the extent to which the modern state is discomposed by, or exploitative of, dissident sexualities. I would say that sexuality is a vastly powerful and conflicted component of any psyche and any social organization, and therefore is always going to figure as a site of struggle. Quite how such struggles will be aligned depends on particular circumstances. We should not expect a consistent relation between, say, fellatio and the military. Rather, divergent accounts are able to adduce evidence from various quarters. There are places where state toleration of some gay practices is under threat (parts of Africa), and others where it is increasing (parts of Europe). In the latter case, Binnie makes nothing of the British Home Office decision in Tony Blair's first administration, allowing lesbians and gay men to bring into the UK an established partner from overseas. In some other places, especially the United States, toleration is both increasing and diminishing. The state is, anyway, not the only relevant institution: we should also be addressing churches, businesses, armies, schools, the press, informal communities of work and neighbouhood. Some of these are local, some global, some both.

While stressing the variability of relations between sexualities and the global body politic, I do not mean to fall back into a naive empiricism, in which each instance speaks only of itself. Binnie, like most commentators, insists that postcolonial peoples are actors in their relation to metropolitan pressures, as well as acted upon. This is surely correct: embedded local customs are not easily overthrown by the sugar and caffeine buzz of cola (which might be less attractive if clean drinking water was more conveniently available). However, this emphasis on elements of resistance leads Binnie into a model of relations that recognizes, primarily, the ways individuals (aspire to) occupy space. He is much less concerned with the sexiness of the organizations that propel and restrain such occupancies. He offers no discussion of the Washington Agenda (the World Bank, the International Monetary Fund, the G8 meetings); business is normally cited as Coca Cola and McDonald's (rather than oil and armaments). Binnie distances himself, shrewdly, from the facile cosmopolitanism that is cultivated in some New Labour circles. Notwithstanding, he tends to see a Blair world in which individuals make wise or foolish choices, and are rewarded and punished accordingly.

At one point Binnie remarks: "Those attending events such as the Gay Games are the people driving the globalization processes" (p. 128). Perhaps this is carelessly written, but it appears to disclose a surprisingly relaxed estimate of the processes we are experiencing. The unstable mixture of attraction and repulsion in First and Third World relations is of course focused uniquely by September 11th, and the invasion of Afghanistan, and subsequently of Iraq. Oddly, Binnie doesn't discuss September 11th, though he references sources from the following year (2002). He makes no mention of the specificities of gender and sexuality among Islamic peoples, nor of key points of intersection between them and the metropolitan sex/gender system.

Without September 11th and the extreme US response, Binnie is able to show something of what is at stake for people who migrate, but he hardly touches on the desperation and intensity that inspire nonmetropolitan people to resist, and embrace, globalization. Nor does he address the inability of the US and its satellite states to appreciate that they may be provoking, however disproportionately, the resistance. The most disturbing ideas arise from the element of sexual humiliation in the torture at Guantanomo Bay and Abu Ghraib. It is a commonplace that sadism and masochism are two sides of the same coin: we need to entertain the thought that the resort to extreme and illogical violence by the US is not just feared, condemned and despised in the rest of the world, but part of the attraction of "America."

Generally, outside metropolitan contexts, sexual dissidence is perceived, centrally, as to do with gender identity – rather than object choice (Binnie doesn't pick this up explicitly). This is true in famous instances, such as the Native American berdache, the Indian hijras and the Brazilian travestis. It is cross – dressing and other transgender signals that ignite enthusiasm and condemnation. What "America" then supplies, internationally, is imagery for the reclamation of sexual dissidence as masculine. You can be queer and manly in the American quasimilitary stance – boots, denim, T-shirts, leather, forage caps. You can assert aggression, muscularity and a principled insensitivity to other people. From such a stance you can bombard civilians and rape detainees.

Not only are there gays in the military: the military is infiltrating gays. In fantasy, few of us are unaffected by these signatures of global power. Yet Binnie concludes a chapter on the politics of migration and tourism with this thought: "One should strive for the eradication of all power relations and inequalities between sexual partners, whether in the west or the developing world" (pp. 105–6) . Should one? Should we expect to transform the entire global sex/gender system with good intentions? And, until that is accomplished, do we really want to limit ourselves to partners where equality is in prospect? Is not power disparity precisely what people are looking for when they explore interracial sexual experiences, as when they cultivate differences of age and class? Should we not seize opportunities to address and embrace the psychic and political dangers of hierarchy, even at the cost of revisiting lineaments of imperialism?

CULTURAL POLITICS

NOTES TO CONTRIBUTORS

- Articles should be approximately 5,000 to 8,000 words (but not exceeding 8,000 words in length unless by prior agreement please).
- They must include a three-sentence biography of the author(s) and an abstract.
- Interviews should also include an author biography.
- Exhibition and book reviews are normally 1,000 words in length but review articles can be between 1,000 and 5,000 words.
- The Publishers will require a disk as well as a hard copy of any contributions.

From time to time, *Cultural Politics* plans to produce special issues devoted to a single topic with a guest editor. Persons wishing to organize a topical issue are invited to submit a proposal which contains a 500-word description of the topic together with a list of potential contributors and paper subjects. Proposals are accepted only after a review by the Journal editors and in-house editorial staff at Berg Publishers.

MANUSCRIPTS

- Manuscripts should be submitted to:
  Dr John Armitage, Co-editor, *Cultural Politics*, School of Arts & Social Sciences, Northumbria University, Newcastle upon Tyne, NE1 8ST UK or to j.armitage@unn.ac.uk
- Manuscripts will be acknowledged and entered into the review process discussed below.
- Manuscripts without illustrations will not be returned unless the author provides a self-addressed stamped envelope.
- Submission of a manuscript to the journal will be taken to imply that it is not being considered elsewhere, in the same form, in any language, without the consent of the editor and publisher. It is a condition of acceptance by the editor of a manuscript for publication that the publishers automatically acquire the copyright of the published article throughout the world. *Cultural Politics* does not pay authors for their manuscripts nor does it provide retyping, drawing, or mounting of illustrations.

STYLE

- US spelling and mechanicals are to be used. Authors are advised to consult The Chicago Manual of Style (14th Edition) as a guideline for style. Webster's Dictionary is our arbiter of spelling. We encourage the use of major subheadings and, where appropriate, second-level subheadings.
- Manuscripts submitted for consideration as an article must contain:
  – a title page with the full title of the article, the author(s) name and address
  – a three-sentence biography for each author.
- Do not place the author's name on any other page of the manuscript.

MANUSCRIPT PREPARATION

- Manuscripts must be typed double-spaced (including quotations, notes and references cited), on one side only, with at least one-inch margins on standard paper using a typeface no smaller than 12pts.
- The original manuscript and a copy of the text on disk (please ensure it is clearly marked with the word-processing program that has been used) must be submitted, along with original photographs (to be returned).
- Authors should retain a copy for their records.
- Any necessary artwork must be submitted with the manuscript.

FOOTNOTES

- Footnotes appear as 'Notes' at the end of articles.
- Authors are advised to include footnote material in the text whenever possible.
- Notes are to be numbered consecutively throughout the paper and are to be typed double-spaced at the end of the text
- ***(Please do not use any footnoting or end-noting programs which your software may offer as this text becomes irretrievably lost at the typesetting stage.)***

REFERENCES

- The list of references should be limited to, and inclusive of, those publications actually cited in the text.
- References are to be cited in the body of the text in parentheses with author's last name, the year of original publication, and page number—e.g. (Rouch 1958: 45).
- Titles and publication information appear as 'References' at the end of the article and should be listed alphabetically by author and chronologically for each author.
- References should be written in the following formats:

Lewis, I.M. and C. Besteman. 1998. "Violence in Somalia: an Exchange." *Cultural Anthropology* 13(1): 100–14.

Mayer, E. 1992. "Peru in Deep Trouble: Mario Vargas Llosa's 'Inquest in the Andes' Reexamined." In G.E. Marcus (ed.) *Rereading Cultural Anthropology*, pp.181–219. Durham: Duke University Press.

Stoll, D. 1999. *Rigoberta Menchu and the Story of All Poor Guatemalans*. Boulder: Westview Press.

- Names of journals and publications should appear in full. Film and video information appear as 'Filmography'.
- References cited should be typed double-spaced on a separate page.
- References not presented in the style required will be returned to the author for revision.

TABLES

- All tabular material should be part of a separately numbered series of 'Tables'.
- Each table must be typed on a separate sheet and identified by a short descriptive title.
- Footnotes for tables appear at the bottom of the table.
- Marginal notations on manuscripts should indicate approximately where tables are to appear.

FIGURES

All illustrative material: drawings, maps, diagrams, and photographs should be designated 'Figures'. They must be submitted in a form suitable for publication without redrawing.

- Drawings should be carefully done with India ink on either hard, white, smooth-surfaced board or good quality tracing paper. Ordinarily, computer-generated drawings are not of publishable quality.
- Photographs should be glossy prints and should be numbered on the back to key with captions. Whenever possible, photographs should be 8 × 10 inches.
- The publishers also encourage artwork to be submitted as scanned files (300dpi or above ONLY) on disc or via email.
- All figures should be numbered consecutively.
- All captions should be typed double-spaced on a separate page.
- Marginal notations on manuscripts should indicate approximately where figures are to appear.
- While the editors and publishers will use all reasonable care in protecting all figures submitted, they cannot assume responsibility for their loss or damage. Authors are discouraged from submitting rare or non-replaceable materials. It is the author's responsibility to secure written copyright clearance (for both print and online usage) on all photographs and drawings that are not in the public domain.

CRITERIA FOR EVALUATION

Cultural Politics is a refereed journal. Manuscripts will be accepted only after review by both the editors and anonymous reviewers deemed competent to make professional judgments concerning the quality of the manuscript.

REPRINTS FOR AUTHORS

Twenty-five reprints of author's articles will be provided to the author free of charge. Additional reprints may be purchased upon request.

New Books from  BERG

August 2005
PB 1 84520 358 5   £10.00 $17.95
HB 1 84520 224 4   £16.99 $24.99

September 2005
PB 1 84520 334 8   £9.99 $15.99
HB 1 84520 327 5   £35.00 $60.00

www.bergpublishers.com

Fashion Theory

The Journal of Dress, Body & Culture

Edited by Valerie Steele

Fashion Theory takes as its starting point a definition of 'fashion' as the cultural construction of the embodied identity. It provides an international and interdisciplinary forum for the analysis of cultural phenomena ranging from foot binding to fashion advertising. All articles have solid theoretical underpinnings and are based on original research.

- Free online access for print subscribers
- International coverage
- Heavily illustrated
- Annual special issues
- Exhibition and book reviews

'Way deeper than your average issue of Vogue.
Essential reading for students and fashion historians.'
The Guardian

'Fashion Theory is both chic and serious - yes, and sexy, too. There is much here to interest students of art, history, design, cultural studies, sociology, art history and anthropology.'
Times Higher Education Supplement

Published from 1997 March, June, September, December

20% Discount for new subscribers
ISSN 1362 704X

	Individuals		Institutions	
1-year subscription	~~£45~~	£36	~~£125~~	£100
	~~$75~~	$60	~~$225~~	$180
2-year subscription	~~£72~~	£58	~~£200~~	£160
	~~$120~~	$96	~~$360~~	$288

Please call +44 (0) 1767 604951 to place your order or order online
at www.bergpublishers.com
Please quote order code FTS5

Home Cultures

Edited by Victor Buchli, Alison Clarke and Dell Upton

Home Cultures is an inderdisciplinary journal dedicated to the critical understanding of the domestic sphere, its artifacts, spaces and relations across timeframes and cultures. Whether as a concept or a physical space, 'home' is a highly fluid and contested site of human existence that reflects and reifies identities and values.

- Free online access for print subscribers
- International coverage
- Heavily illustrated

'Home Cultures [shows] the crucial importance of domestic space to humanity at large.'
Benjamin S. Orlove, University of California Davis

'An innovative scholarly forum for a crucial research area that astonishingly has never yet had its own 'home'.
Don Slater, London School of Economics

Published from 2004 March, July, November

Material Religion

The Journal of objects, art and belief

Edited by David Goa, David Morgan, Crispin Paine and S.Brent Plate

Material Religion seeks to explore how religion happens in material culture - images, devotional and liturgical objects, architecture and sacred space, works of art and mass-produced artifacts. No less important than these material forms are the many different practices that put them to work. Ritual, communication, ceremony, instruction, meditation, propaganda, pilgrimage, display, magic, liturgy and interpretation constitute many of the practices whereby religious material culture constructs the worlds of belief.

- Free online access for print subscribers
- International coverage
- Heavily illustrated

'*Material Religion* will address a much neglected feature of religion, contributing substantially to the understanding of how religion works in people's lives.'
Margaret Miles, The Graduate Theological Union, Berkeley

Published from 2005 March, July, November

20% Discount for new subscribers
ISSN 1743-2200

	Individuals		Institutions	
1-year subscription	~~£44~~	£35	~~£150~~	£120
	~~$72~~	$58	~~$250~~	$200
2-year subscription	~~£70~~	£56	~~£240~~	£192
	~~$115~~	$92	~~$400~~	$320

Please call +44 (0) 1767 604951 to place your order or order online
at www.bergpublishers.com

Please quote order code MAS5